G000270828

FINN &
THE FIANNA

HILLINGDON

WITHDRAWN

BOROUGH LIBRARIES

DANIEL ALLISON

The
History
Press

This book is dedicated to David Campbell,
who introduced me to Finn and
in whom the spirit of the Fianna lives and shines.

Cover illustrations: © Ouroboros Design

First published 2021

The History Press
97 St George's Place,
Cheltenham,
Gloucestershire,
GL50 3QB
www.thehistorypress.co.uk

© Daniel Allison, 2021

The right of Daniel Allison to be identified as the Author
of this work has been asserted in accordance with the
Copyright, Designs and Patents Act 1988.

All rights reserved. No part of this book may be reprinted
or reproduced or utilised in any form or by any electronic,
mechanical or other means, now known or hereafter invented,
including photocopying and recording, or in any information
storage or retrieval system, without the permission in writing
from the Publishers.

British Library Cataloguing in Publication Data.
A catalogue record for this book is available from the British Library.

ISBN 978 0 7509 9144 5

Typesetting and origination by Typo•glyphix, Burton-on-Trent
Printed and bound by TJ Books Limited, Padstow, Cornwall

MIX
Paper from
responsible sources
FSC
www.fsc.org   FSC® C013056

CONTENTS

Foreword   7
Introduction   8
Pronunciation Guide   11

Part I
The Coming of Finn   13
The Fate of Coull   15
The Boyhood of Finn   19
The Salmon of Wisdom   24
Samhain at Tara   30
Bran & Sceolan   36
The Lad of the Skins   45
The Birth of Diarmuid   54
The Giant's Causeway   61
Black, Brown & Grey   66
The Birth of Ossian   75

Part II
The High Days of Finn   83
Dark, Battle & Eagle   85
Finn & the Fool   92
The Daughter of King Under Wave   98
The Cave of Keshcorran   110
The Healing of Caoilte   114
The Red Woman   123
Finn & the Phantoms   129
The Hunt of Slieve Cuillin   135

Part III

Diarmuid & Grainne	141
The Wedding	143
The Wood of Two Huts	152
The Green Champions	158
The Berry Tree	169
The Quarrel	184
The Wanderers	191
The Boar Hunt	200

Part IV

The Last Days of the Fianna	213
The Death of Goll	215
The Last Battle of the Fianna	226
Ossian & Niamh	238
Ossian & Patrick	244
Author's Note	251
Sources	252
Acknowledgements	253

FOREWORD

A flowing stream of story and legend unites Scotland and Ireland. Wherever it bubbles up, the name of Ossian is heard – Ossian the bard, storyteller and musician. But Ossian is the mouthpiece, the fount of a huge family of tales revolving round Finn, Diarmuid, Grainne, Caoilte and many others.

Each of these heroes, and sometimes rogues, dazzles in their own right, but collectively they provide the unfolding saga of an age when the earth was young, nature was close, the ancestors ever near, and magic in the very breath of life.

Now a storyteller of the present day has dipped into that magic, and woven his own spell. Daniel Allison provides a fluid, enchanting telling of the saga, with each key tale eloquently placed. He is respectful of tradition but also an entertainer of today reaching new audiences.

Moreover, these stories have an especial poignancy, a radical edge, in a time when humanity threatens planet earth, and ourselves, with extinction. For the Fianna, the free life of nature is the highest experience and value. Without that there is no life worth the name, just grey existence.

Open this book at any point and tune in to the voice of the storyteller. Then begin where all good stories begin: at the beginning. You will not put this down till the last lovely page has been scanned.

Donald Smith
Director
The Scottish International Storytelling Festival

INTRODUCTION

I earn my living by telling stories. It's the best job in the world. Whenever I tell a tale of the Fianna in a Scottish school, I first ask the pupils if they have heard of Finn MacCoull. They usually look at me blankly.

It's a strange thing to ask. There is no need to ask English children if they have heard of King Arthur or Robin Hood. Most Irish people I meet know Finn and at least a few of the tales. But in Scotland, we have forgotten our heroes. Hopefully, this book will help us to remember.

According to the tales, the Fianna were a warrior band who protected Ireland and Scotland from invaders. Numerous individual Fianna are mentioned in the stories, but most prominent are Finn, his son Ossian, his grandson Oscar and his friend Diarmuid, along with his rivals, Goll and Conan. While a good number of stories survive, it is likely that these are only a fraction of those that once existed. The ones that we have are so wonderful that we shouldn't feel too hard done by.

The tales of the Fianna are one of the four cycles of Irish mythology, which are usually placed in the following order: the Mythological Cycle, the Ulster Cycle, the Fenian (Fianna) Cycle and the Cycle of Kings. The Mythological Cycle tells of the coming to Ireland of the Tuatha De Danaan, the Children of Danu, better known nowadays as the fairy folk or sidhe. They took Ireland and ruled it until the Gaels came, pushing the sidhe over the sea and into their ever-bright underground halls.

The Ulster Cycle is the story of the mighty warrior Cuchulainn and the War for the Brown Bull of Cooley. The sidhe do feature in these tales, but mostly they remain in the background; the emphasis is firmly on men. The Cycle of Kings deals in part with real, historical kings.

The Fianna cycle is placed after the Ulster Cycle, but it might be better placed after the Mythological Cycle. There is a huge emphasis in the Fianna tales on movement between the world of men and the supernatural world of the sidhe. The wild forests, beaches and mountains often act as gateways to the otherworld. As Donald Smith writes, 'For the Fianna, the free life of nature is the highest experience and value. Without that there is no life worth the name, just grey existence'. The Ulster Knights are more modern; above all, they love gold and battle-won glory.

When entering the otherworld, Finn and his men often have to use their wit as well as their strength to survive, and in turn come back rewarded with new knowledge, abilities and magical items. In this respect, the tales very much resemble those of animistic hunter-gather societies such as those of Siberia. This leads me to wonder if the tales of the Fianna do not go back to the earliest inhabitants of Ireland and Scotland, who settled after the glaciers of the last ice age retreated.

It is a long time since that world passed away; in the time since then the tales have changed. Lady Gregory's *Gods and Fighting Men*, published in 1904, has the Fianna as an Iron Age war band that runs a kind of protection racket, demanding so much gold of the kings and lords of Ireland that they eventually rebel and make war upon them. Before that, in the 1760s, James Macpherson helped usher in the Romantic era by publishing *The Works of Ossian*, which he claimed were his translation of ancient Gaelic tales. The works were wildly popular; Napoleon is said to have slept with a copy under his pillow. Bitter controversy erupted when it emerged that Macpherson may have written the poems himself, or at least wildly embellished the originals.

In recent years, writers such as Marie Heaney, George Macpherson, David Campbell and Eddie Lenihan have written down the tales. I have added my voice with the aim of bringing the principal stories and a number of outliers together in one volume, as a complete cycle from beginning to end. Of course, stories in a pre-literate society were never brought together and made to fit; there would have been many that contradicted one another. I have tried to find a balance between allowing the stories to strike disparate tones while emphasising the threads of continuity that make them a whole.

I don't claim that this book is the last word on the Fianna. There are elements of dialogue, description, location and character here that are my own envisioning of the tales. If you are curious, I would urge you to seek out other tellers of these stories and build up your own picture of the Fianna. And if you love the stories, don't just read them; tell them. Between the mouth of the storyteller and the ear of the listener is a doorway to the otherworld; it is where stories truly come alive.

PRONUNCIATION GUIDE

Aodh Fada of Eamhuin	Ayd Fada of <u>Eh</u>-wan
Ath-Luain	Ath-<u>Loo</u>-an
Beinn Builen	Ben <u>Bool</u>-ben
Beinn Edair	Ben <u>Edd</u>-ir
Beinn Sgritheall	Ben <u>Shreh</u>-hal
Bodhmall	<u>Bauw</u>-mal
Boinn	<u>Boyn</u>
Cairell	Cairell
Caoilte	<u>Kweel</u>-cha
Cliodhna	<u>Klee</u>-uh-na
Cnuca	Kih-<u>noh</u>-cha
Coull	<u>Coo</u>-hl
Crochnuit	<u>Croch</u>-noot
Cuillin	<u>Coo</u>-lin
Doire-da-Bhoth	<u>Doy</u>-ra da Bhoth
Dubh	Doovh
Duibhne	Doon
Eoghan	<u>Oh</u>-in
Fiachu	Fi-<u>ah</u>-koo
Fianna	<u>Fi</u>-anna
Finn	Fyonn or Fin
Finnachaidh	<u>Fee</u>-na-ha
Fomorians	Fo-<u>mo</u>-rians
Gabhra	<u>Gav</u>-ra

Glen Lyon	Glen Lion
Goibniu	<u>Gov</u>-noo
Grainne	<u>Gronn</u>-ya
Iollan	<u>Ull</u>-an
Leinster	<u>Lenn</u>-ster
Liath Luachra	<u>Lee</u>-ha <u>Lu</u>-chra
Lugaidh	<u>Loo</u>-ah
Muadhan	Moo<u>wa</u>-dan
Mannanan	Man-<u>an</u>-awn
Muirne	<u>Myrr</u>-na
Niamh	Neevh
Ossian	O-<u>sheen</u>
Oweynagat	<u>Oh</u>wey-na-<u>ga</u>
Sabha	<u>Sav</u>-ha
Samhain	<u>Sow</u>-in (sow as in cow)
Sceolan	Shkee-<u>o</u>-lan
Slieve Luachra	Sleeve <u>Loo</u>-chra
Sidhe	Shee
Suchet	<u>Soo</u>-shay
Teig	Tayg
Tir Nan Nog	<u>Tier</u> Na-<u>Noag</u>
Tuatha De Danaan	<u>Too</u>-a Day <u>Dan</u>-an
Tuiren	<u>Tirr</u>-en
Uchtdealb	<u>Ucht</u>-djalv

PART I

THE COMING OF FINN

THE FATE OF COULL

Long ago, in a time when the veils between the worlds were thinner than they are now, there lived in the wilds of Ireland and Scotland a band of warriors called the Fianna. It was their job to guard those lands against the men and monsters who would invade them. When the shores of their beloved homelands were safe, the Fianna would feast, fight and make their own trouble.

Coull was the leader of the Fianna. He was tall, fair, open-hearted and open-handed. His heart belonged to a maiden named Muirne, who loved him as he loved her.

Muirne was the daughter of Teig, Chief Druid to the High King of Ireland. You might have expected Teig to see Coull, the renowned Captain of the Fianna, as a fine match for his daughter. But it was not so. For the Fianna, admired as they were, were wild men. They lived their lives and made their beds beneath the boughs of trees, at the ocean's edge, in the high hill's shadow. They had dealings with the sidhe, whom some call the fairy folk; their trade was in battle, in blood and iron. In short, they did not always make good husbands.

Coull came to Teig's dwelling, a shining white fort on the Hill of Allen, and offered his suit. Teig refused him. Coull left and when Teig was next gone, he returned, climbing over the wall as the fort glistened in the moonlight. He found Muirne, kissed her and led her away into the wild woods.

Deep into the forest they went. By a waterfall pool they bound their hands together and exchanged vows of love. In beech-dappled light and to the blackbird's song they loved and laughed and fell into one another, knowing their time would be over soon.

Teig discovered his daughter had been taken. Storms shook Ireland as the druid raged. He went to Tara, seat of the High King, and demanded that the sword of justice strike Coull. The High King was reluctant.

'Coull is my friend,' he said, 'and the Fianna are a force to be feared.'

'If you do not move against Coull,' said Teig, 'I will speak druid-words against your name.'

The King quivered at that. Even he was not immune to a druid's curse. He called a meeting of his most trusted men, and set his power against the power of Coull.

War drums resounded at Tara. Battle-horns blew from east to west. Messengers crossed the country as fighting men took the road to Tara, where a great camp soon spread across the plain.

Among the King's forces were a group of Fianna disloyal to Coull. These were the Sons of Morna. Chief amongst them was Suchet, a tall, fierce and cunning warrior whom his brothers both loved and feared. His chief henchmen were bald-headed Conan and quick-tongued Black Gary. The High King promised Suchet that if he brought down Coull, he would be made Captain of the Fianna.

Coull and Muirne emerged from the forest. Around Coull the Fianna rallied and soon their army was ready to march. On the Plain of Cnuca, where the City of Dublin now sits, the two armies met.

For the first time, men of the Fianna faced one another across the battlefield.

It would not be the last time.

⚬⚬⚬

The sword-hour came. Spears were rattled, shields were beaten by grim-faced warriors ready for slaughter. Though the sun shone upon them, they knew this day was a dark one.

Ravens gathered in the air, hungry for the feast.

Coull took from his belt the Dord Fiann, the horn of the Fianna. He blew upon it, Suchet's horn answered and the battle began. Soon the grass was red and littered with corpses as the Fianna fought their brothers.

Amid the chaos of the battle, Suchet spied Coull. He called to Black Gary and the two of them fought their way through the melee until no man stood between Suchet and Coull.

Coull attacked. Suchet answered his strike and the two greatest warriors of the Fianna fought. For all Suchet's size, strength and cunning, he was not a match for Coull. The quick-armed Captain slipped like a ghost through Suchet's attacks and lunged forward. Suchet pulled back but was not quick enough. Coull's sword pierced his eye. Suchet was thereafter known as Goll, or 'Blind', Mac Morna.

Coull would have won then, but for Black Gary. As Suchet roared in pain, Black Gary threw himself against Coull from behind. Coull stumbled and it was all Suchet needed. He swung his sword and cut Coull's head from his body.

'Coull is dead!' went up the cry. It carried across the plain, and soon Coull's forces were in rout, running for the forest that bordered the plain.

⚬⚬⚬

The King's forces cheered. Dark liquid streaming from his eye, Suchet laughed. The battle was won.

But what of Muirne?

Watching from the woods that bordered the battlefield, Muirne saw her lover slain. She retreated, heart-riven, into the forest. In a sunlit glade she fell to her knees and keened for Coull. Days and nights passed as she sang the death-song of the golden-haired, gentle-hearted warrior. Coull would never know his own child; the child growing within her.

When the first agonies of her grief had passed, Muirne made her way home to the Hill of Allen. Teig would not open his gates to her. He came to the rampart and called her shameful names until she turned and walked away.

Muirne took another road. Travelling by night lest the Sons of Morna were after her, she made her way to the house of two druid-women, Liath Luachra and Bodhmall. These women were friends of hers, and they kept her hidden in their home until her son was born.

She named the boy Finn. Muirne was full of joy at her son's birth, but she was fearful too. Coull's son was a threat to Goll, and if Goll learnt of Finn's existence, he would surely kill him.

All night the three women talked as Muirne held her son to her chest. At last they came to an agreement. Muirne would leave her son with them and seek out a new life over the waves. Meanwhile, Liath Luachra and Bodhmall would take the boy into the wilds and raise him, keeping him hidden from those who would destroy him.

So it was that Muirne said goodbye to her son and left Ireland, a gown of grief heavy upon her shoulders. Finn's foster mothers left their house and made for the deep, deep woods.

THE BOYHOOD OF FINN

Among the hills and woods of Slieve Bloom, Finn's foster mothers made a new home. Finn grew up not among warriors and weapons but among oak and beech, hazel and ash, deer and squirrels and winding streams. His world was peaceful and he knew that Liath Luachra and Bodhmall loved him. His mother was a fleeting shadow in his thoughts; he did not know what a father was.

Finn grew older.

He wandered the woods around their hut until he knew every tree, every stone and every bend in the stream. He went further, finding and extending the boundaries of his world. Finn gazed in wonder at his discoveries: dragonflies and newts, tadpoles and corncrakes, a snuffling badger emerging from her set.

He learnt the songs of the birds, climbing into the treetops to join the dawn chorus. He stared up at the stars, giving them names and stories as he traced their slow voyage through the night.

Finn grew older.

❧

As Finn grew older he asked more and more questions. He wanted to know why the seasons changed, what came after death and where the stars landed when they fell from the sky. By the fire at night, nestled among furs beneath their rough roof, Liath Luachra and Bodhmall told him of the world.

❧

'This land is called Ireland,' said Liath Luachra, the huntress. 'It is surrounded by the sea, a great plain made of water that cannot be drunk. Ireland is divided into four provinces: Leinster, Connacht, Munster and Ulster. Each province has its King, and the High King of Ireland rules over them all.'

'Over the sea, to the west, are islands where the Fomorians dwell,' said Bodhmall, the druid. 'Some of them have the shape of men. Others have the heads of men and the bodies of beasts, or the heads of beasts and the bodies of men. There are even those that dwell beneath the sea.'

'Many lands lie to the east,' said Liath Luachra. 'The place that the folk of Ireland love best is Alba, the land of storms where legions of mountains pierce the sky.'

'What is beneath the earth?' asked Finn.

Bodhmall smiled. 'The Tuatha De Danaan,' she answered.

So Finn learnt of the Tuatha De Danaan, the Children of Danu, who had taken Ireland from a people called the Firbolgs and ruled her until the day his own people came.

On that day, the Tuatha De Danaan had their druids call a storm from the sky, so that the Gaels, Finn's ancestors, could not land their ships. But the Gaels had a mighty druid called Amergin, who spoke a poem that silenced the storm. The Gaels landed and took Ireland for their own. The Tuatha De Danaan, sometimes called the fairies or sidhe, made new homes in underground halls or went over the sea to Tir Nan Nog, Land of the Ever-Young.

Night after night Finn learnt of the world. That which he learnt, he never forgot. He loved best the tales of the Children of Danu, who lived long lives beneath the earth and could be beautiful or monstrous, kind or cruel. Finn fashioned his own tales of Goibniu the Smith and dreamed of the Morrigan, the Mother of Battles whose crows fed on the slain. He pretended he was Manannan, riding his white horse over the waves, or that he was Angus Og, brandishing twin swords and twin spears.

Of Coull, and the Fianna, Finn never heard a word.

Finn grew older. He hunted with Liath Luachra by day. After Liath Luachra had fallen asleep each night, Finn lay awake, watching Bodhmall as she gazed into the fire, seeing things unseen by Finn and singing her druid-songs.

❧

Day by day Finn grew taller and stronger. He thought always of the world beyond the forest and yearned to explore it. His foster mothers would not let him, and when he asked them why not, they fell silent.

A rift grew between them and Finn as he sensed knowledge being withheld from him. Rebelliousness took root and he wandered farther from home than was allowed. Thus Finn arrived one day at the edge of a field.

He had never seen such a thing. Nor had he seen such a thing as the grassy common, or the village beyond, or the boys out playing a game on the common. He approached them, and asked what game they were playing, and could he join in?

The boys weren't keen. They didn't know who this wild-eyed stranger was. There was something about him that marked him as different to them, and that made them uneasy. But they explained that the game was called hurley and showed him how to play. He was given a stick and was soon running beside them as they hit the ball and, more often, each other.

Finn was good at the game. In fact, he was so good that he was soon demanding that they all play together against him, as otherwise it was too easy and boring.

They accepted. Finn beat them single-handedly. The boys lost their tempers, abandoned the ball and beat Finn with their sticks. He broke free and ran away, disappearing into the forest.

Finn decided not to tell Liath Luachra and Bodhmall about the encounter. Yet as the days went by he found that he couldn't stop

❧

thinking about those boys. They had made it clear that they didn't want to be friends with him, but he wanted so much to learn their games, their names and their ways. So he made up his mind to seek them out.

He found them playing in a river pool, leaping and diving from the surrounding rocks. Emerging from the woods, Finn asked if could play.

'Oh yes,' said the biggest of the boys. 'You can play with us.'

Finn grinned, took off his shirt and boots and dived into the water. The moment he broke the water's surface, he heard shouting and felt hands pressing on his head and shoulders. The boys swarmed over him, holding him under.

Rage took Finn. He broke free, leapt upon the biggest boy's back and pushed him under. Another boy came at him and he leapt onto the shoulders of that boy. Soon Finn was leaping back and forth, stamping on the backs of the boys as he held them all underwater at once.

After enough of his rage was spent, Finn leapt to the bank. He grabbed his shirt and boots and ran away again.

This time he told his foster mothers what had happened. They were worried.

'Finn,' said Liath Luachra, 'you mustn't do such things. Stories will be told about you.'

'So what if they are?' asked Finn.

A look passed between the two women.

'Because of who you are, Finn MacCoull,' said Bodhmall.

Finn found his answers that night. He wept with pride and sorrow as he heard of his mother's beauty and kindness, and as he learnt of his father, Coull, the Captain of the Fianna. His sadness turned to anger as he was told of the Battle of Cnuca and the day his father died.

'I know you will want vengeance, Finn,' said Liath Luachra. 'But we promised your mother we would keep you hidden. For her sake, stay with us.'

Finn did not want to stay. The world was calling to him; his beloved forest had become a prison. Yet he promised he would he stay.

Perhaps Finn would have honoured his promise and stayed in Slieve Bloom. He might have broken it and gone out in search of Goll. In the end, the choice was not his. For a story was spreading across Ireland, about a mysterious golden-haired child who lived in the forests of Slieve Bloom.

Goll MacMorna heard the tale. He knew at once who this must be: the Son of Coull.

Goll would suffer no threat to his rule. The boy had to die.

Days later, a hand-picked force of Goll's men made their way into Slieve Bloom. They found the little hut where Finn, Liath Luachra and Bodhmall lived.

But Finn and his foster mothers had already left.

THE SALMON
OF WISDOM

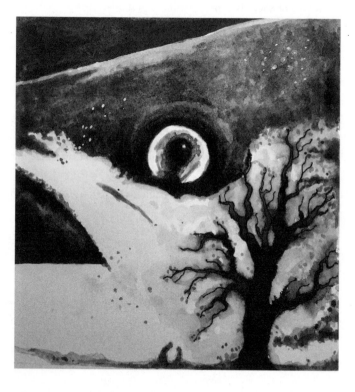

They parted ways. Those women were wise enough to know that
Finn had stepped on to the path of destiny. So they sent him on his
way, with their blessing and with two pieces of advice. One: never
to go by the name of Finn, Son of Coull. Two: to seek out Finegas,
the poet, who dwelt on the banks of the Boyne.

Finn made his way across the country. He hunted for his supper, slept upon leaves and avoided places where people dwelt. He went south, north, east and west, and when his heart grew lonely he would stop at a campfire, taking his fill of news and good cheer before slipping away into the night. Always he asked which way lay the River Boyne. One day, he reached its banks.

He had been told that Finegas dwelt by a pool, far upriver; so upriver Finn went. On and on, by sun and moon, shivers of anticipation rattling him as open fields gave way to thick forest and the river grew narrower, faster, fiercer.

One night, as the moon poured its light upon the silvery forest, Finn reached a pool. He was tired and hungry, for since reaching the river he had neither eaten nor slept; but his tiredness and hunger were forgotten as he gazed at the scene before him.

The pool was still. So still that the stars shone, mirrored, upon its silent surface. Rushes crowded around its edges, leaning in as if to catch some hidden murmur. Nine hazelnut trees surrounded the pool, their branches in a tangled embrace.

At first, Finn didn't see him.

He sat as still as a being of stone. His gnarled, weather-beaten hands rested on his lap, among the folks of his mossy cloak; his white beard snaked down to dangle over the edge of the water.

'Finegas,' said Finn.

The old poet did not move. He simply went on staring into the pool. So Finn looked too, but saw nothing except black water and stars.

A hazelnut fell into the pool.

'Do you know what these tree are, boy?' asked Finegas.

'They're hazel trees,' answered Finn.

'They are hazel trees. And from them grow the nuts of wisdom. Those nuts fall into the pool, as you have seen.'

'What happens to them?'

'They are eaten,' said Finegas, 'by the salmon of wisdom. For more years than you have lived I have sat here, awaiting the day when I will catch that fish, cook him, eat him and finally possess all knowledge.'

'I am Demne. I will help you,' said Finn.

Finegas looked the lad over. He must have liked the look of Finn, for he said, 'Very well. Go and make a fire. Cook something for our supper, and make a bed for yourself.'

Finn did as he was bidden. He made a fire, he made something for their supper, and when that was done he made a bed of leaves and lay down.

There at the salmon's pool, he remained.

Autumn came, and still Finn remained. Winter came, and spring and summer, and Finn had not left Finegas. Finn took care of the hunting, the cooking, the mending of clothes and all the others things that needed done. Finegas was pleased, for this left him free to get on with his fishing.

Finegas would fish all day, and sometimes all night. On some moonlit evenings, he would go to the pool without his fishing rod. Finn followed him one time. He saw the salmon's head rise from the pool as Finegas approached the water.   Finegas waded into the shallows and the two adversaries circled one another, their heads moving in slow, artful patterns. It seemed to Finn to be a dance of war and a dance of friendship.

When he wasn't fishing, Finegas would talk with Finn. Finn asked Finegas why he wanted all knowledge, and Finegas replied that he wanted it for the sake of poetry, and poetry alone.

'There is,' said Finegas, 'no higher art than the weaving of words.'

Years passed. But for the changing weather, every day was like the last.

Then, one cold, windy day in autumn, Finegas caught the salmon.

❀

Finn had risen early. He went out to hunt and returned with a rabbit. He put wood on the fire, walked down to the pool and there!

Finegas was stood on the bank, his rod clasped in his hands. His eyes were bulging, his chest heaving and on the end of his rod, the salmon of wisdom was thrashing. It was so big that it might have eaten Finegas, pulled him underwater or knocked him senseless with a slap of its tail. Finn feared for his mentor. Should he help?

'Stay back, lad!' shouted Finegas. 'This is between the two of us.'

Finn watched as the fish bucked and pulled. Finegas held on, giving no ground. He was like an oak; ancient, rooted, immovable.

Eventually, the salmon's thrashing slowed. It merely flopped and then ceased even that. Finegas pulled it in.

As he did so, for just a moment, the fish looked at Finn before its eyes went still.

Finn helped Finegas lift the salmon onto the bank, laying it down on a bed of rushes. The old man cried. He reached down and stroked its scales.

'Boy,' he said, 'I am tired. I will need you to cook the fish for me.'

So Finn dragged the great salmon to their nearby camp. He built up the fire and made a great spit upon which the fish would turn. When that was done, and with some difficulty, he put the fish upon the spit and sat there, turning the spit, listening to the crackle of the salmon's sizzling flesh and the sobbing of Finegas, who still sat by the pool.

The day passed. Finn turned the spit; slowly the salmon cooked. He stared into its lifeless eyes and wondered if Finegas would miss his adversary, his muse, his friend.

The flesh of the salmon was giving off a sweet smell; it was almost cooked. Finn realised he too was mourning the ancient fish.

The sun was setting in a shower of gold. The salmon was sizzling and smelling ever more sweet.

A bubble of liquid formed upon its flesh.

It grew, and grew, and burst.

Boiling liquid flew from the bubble, and a drop of the liquid landed on Finn's thumb.

Finn put his thumb into his mouth to cool it, touching his thumb to his tooth.

He froze.

He realised what he had done.

And he realised more than that.

Much, much more.

In that moment, like a tidal wave that covers the land and tears apart everything in its path, all knowledge was revealed to Finn. He heard the muttering of the trees and the songs of the stars. He felt the beating wings of every bird in the sky. The great beasts of the seabed gazed into his eyes; sun-fire burned in his blood. Finn knew every mind's desire, walked every heart's hidden roads. He witnessed the birth and death of gods.

Finn took his finger from his mouth. He was back in the forest; he was Finn again.

Should he tell Finegas about this? Best not. Finegas might be angry that he had tasted the salmon. It was an accident, after all. No need to mention it. So Finn walked the short distance from their camp to the pool, where Finegas, rose, turned, looked at him … and frowned.

His frown became a dark stare.

'You have tasted the salmon,' said Finegas.

'Yes,' said Finn.

Finegas smiled. 'Of course you have,' he said. 'For the salmon was always meant for you, Finn, Son of Coull.'

Finn was stunned. 'But … what will I do with this knowledge?' he asked.

'That is up to you,' said Finegas. 'Though I would ask that you give at least some of yourself to the making of poetry.'

'What will you do?' asked Finn.

'There is nothing more for me to do,' said Finegas. 'Good-bye, Finn.' And with that the old poet turned and walked away into the forest.

Finn left the camp the next morning, shouldering his pack and walking through the forest before the light came. He walked until he reached the edge of a lake, and there he sat and spoke to the dawn.

> The sun is singing the world awake.
> I, Finn, am the sun.
> The moon has turned her back to the world;
> I am the darkness that swallows her.
>
> I am the serpents beneath the world,
> Jewelled cities within their coils.
> I am the man who first met death,
> A thousand lifetimes ago.
>
> The earth beneath his feet I am,
> The cold breath upon his lips;
> And the rolling of thunder, the beating of drums
> In star-lit halls where the sidhe folk dance.
>
> The King of Floods dreams me in his hall.
> The Mother of Battles fed me to her crows.
> I shall sit by this lake, until the end of all worlds,
> And when all else is gone, I shall remain.

After speaking these words, Finn sat a while longer. Then he rose and headed east towards Tara, to find Goll MacMorna and claim his inheritance.

SAMHAIN AT TARA

The Hill of Tara, seat of the High King of Ireland, was ablaze with the light of a thousand fires. It was Samhain, the night when the old year meets the new, and the scene was set for a feast.

Kings and lords, druids and bards, warriors and word-weavers converged upon the great hill in Ireland's east. In their finest array they made their way to the feasting hall, where tables groaned under the weight of meat and mead, whisky and ale. Each took their place, as near to the High King as their station allowed, and smiled as they sat down and greeted their neighbours. Yet their smiles faded quickly.

The High King stood. The feasters stood. The High King drank, the feasters drank and the feast was under way. Bright harp notes sung through the air, knives cut through meat and cups clashed together. Yet every jest and merry song rang false, and babes in their mothers' arms howled like wolves.

The guards on the gate spied a figure on the road. He drew close, and they saw that though he was young, there was nobility in his bearing and wisdom in his blue eyes. Though they did not know him, they let him pass, and watched him until he was out of sight. There was something about this young man.

The young man, of course, was Finn, who had come to claim his inheritance.

Finn entered the feasting hall and walked through the throng until he stood by the High King's table.

The High King looked up. His eyes met Finn's.

'Who are you?' asked the King.

'My name is Finn, Son of Coull,' said Finn.

'Son of Coull?'

'Yes.'

The King looked at Finn a while longer. He looked at the men sat on either side of him. Then he took a horn of mead and put it in Finn's hand.

'You are welcome,' he said. A seat was found for Finn, and placed at the King's side.

Finn sat, sipped his mead and looked around.

Sat on the far side of the King was a giant warrior. His hair was long and curled, his muscles strained at the confines of his clothes and he was regarding Finn intently, with a single eye.

This man was surely Goll MacMorna. The warrior who over-threw Finn's father; but not before Coull took his eye.

Sat on the far side of Goll was another mountain of a man. This one was bald; his face was ugly and surly, yet curiously comical.

This was surely Conan MacMorna, Goll's brother.

Another warrior sat at the King's table. This one was not so much a mountain as a tall tree, or even a rod of lightning. His hair was grey and his features sharp, as if shaped by the scouring of the wind. He was smiling gently at Finn.

This was surely Caoilte, his father's friend and the fastest runner of the Fianna.

Finn attended to his fare. He pretended not to notice the looks passing between Goll and Conan. Clearly Finn's appearance had been a great surprise to them, and clearly they did not know what to do about it.

The feast went on until its fire began to fade, at which time Finn put a question to the King.

'Sire,' he said, 'this is a magnificent feast. Though I am inexperienced in feasting, I am sure no better feast will be given anywhere in Ireland tonight. Even if it were, those present would not be in the company of the High King. Why, then, does the company seem ill at ease?'

'You have a keen eye, Son of Coull,' said the King. 'I will tell you why. The company are mournful for the Samhain feast at Tara is cursed.

'Each year, a fairy man comes from Sidhe Finnachaidh to this feast. The first we know of his presence is the sound of his harp, that cuts through all other sounds; and that is the last we know of his presence. For at the sound of his harp, all fall asleep as fast as the kestrel plummets.'

'And what happens then?' asked Finn.

'Then,' said the King, 'he sets the feasting hall afire. We awaken only when the flames lick our boots. The air fills with screams as we try to escape, and not all succeed. Yet still we come here to feast each year, for it will not be said that the great men and women of Ireland are cowards.'

'That is a terrible fate,' said Finn.

'It is,' said the King, 'and so I make this proclamation.' He rose to his feet and raised his voice; the hall quickly fell silent. 'I proclaim that whoever delivers us from the man of the sidhe,' and here he glanced quickly at Finn, 'will have his inheritance, be it big or small.'

Finn rose to his feet.

'That person is me,' he said. 'I will deliver you from the fairy man of Sidhe Finnachaidh.'

There was uproar at this. All vied to see who had spoken; many scoffed when they saw the young man who made such a claim. Others, though, remarked on his resemblance to Coull.

While the hubbub went on, a warrior approached Finn.

'I can see you are Coull's son,' said the warrior. 'I will help you defeat the fairy man. Take this.' He handed Finn a spear. 'When you hear his music, touch the spear to your forehead. When you have him in sight, strike him down with it.'

Finn thanked the warrior, who gave his name as Fiacha. He left the hall, spear in hand.

❦

❦

Finn walked among the houses and storehouses of Tara. It was deepest night now. The air was sharp and the stars bright. Finn guessed that the fairy man was near.

Beneath an oak tree Finn sat down to wait.

He waited.

Soon, Finn heard the sweet sound of a harp being struck.

So wonderfully did the fairy man play that for a moment Finn almost allowed himself to listen. Instead he took the spear and put its tip to his forehead – and not a moment too soon. For his eyelids were already drooping, his head nodding to the soft caress of the sidhe man's music.

Finn fell asleep.

It was the shortest sleep he ever took. The spear's tip struck his brow, his head snapped back and Finn rose, ready for the hunt.

Down darkened pathways Finn trod until he turned a corner and spied the fairy man. Gleefully the little sidhe strode this way and that way, chuckling and chirping to himself as he played. He did not notice Finn.

Finn followed him all the way to the feasting hall.

Outside the doors, the fairy man stopped and began to pluck a new tune. Finn wept at its beauty while inside the hall, the carousing gave way to murmuring, then silence.

The fairy man ceased his plucking. He hoisted his harp over his shoulder.

Finn circled the sidhe. Silently he stalked through the shadows as the fairy man drew in a deep breath. He breathed in deeper, and deeper, his belly bulging as his skin and eyes began to glow and black smoke poured from his mouth.

The sidhe dropped to all fours, lunged forward and belched a torrent of fire, aimed at the hall doors.

It was met by Finn.

Before the doors Finn leapt. As the flames shot towards him he held up his cloak to meet them. The sidhe-fire struck Finn's cloak and did not melt it; for Finn spoke words that made it shimmer and soak up the flames as if they were water.

The fairy man was enraged. He snarled at Finn, drew in another breath and released a blast twice as terrible as the last. Finn's cloak absorbed it all. The fairy man blew again, and again, until his torrents of fire shrank, stuttered and finally died.

Finn let go of his cloak. It fell to the ground and disappeared into the earth, taking the fairy man's fires with it.

Finn smiled at the sidhe and put his hand on his sword hilt.

The fairy man turned and ran.

Down the hill he ran, whimpering in panic. He passed through the gates and turned north towards his home. Finn pursued. The fairy man was swift, yet Finn was as swift. Across Ireland he pursued his prey, over hills and through forests, until they came to the hill of Sidhe Finnachaidh.

The fairy man shot up the slopes. Finn grit his teeth as he fought to keep up.

A strange howl came from the fairy man. Up ahead of him, Finn saw a chink of light appear in the hillside that widened as a door into the hill opened. A figure stood within the doorway, beckoning the sidhe forward as he cackled and whooped; he was almost home safe.

Finn stopped. Aimed. Threw his spear.

The fairy man was crossing the threshold as Finn's spear struck him, piercing his heart.

Back at Tara, as the fires of dawn awoke in the east, the High King of Ireland and all his company awoke in their seats or upon the hall's floor. They rose, looked about themselves and remarked with great pleasure that they were alive, the hall undamaged.

The King led them outside to look for signs of what had happened. Down the path to the gates they went, and there they were met by Finn.

The Son of Coull was leaning against the gates of Tara, Fiacha's spear in his hand and a satisfied smile upon his face. Above the gates, on a high wooden pole, was the head of the fairy of Sidhe Finnachaidh.

The High King led Finn, Caoilte and Goll into a counsel room.

'Goll,' said the King. 'I give you a choice now. You are no longer Captain of the Fianna. You may leave Tara today with my payment, thanks and blessing, and go over the sea to seek your fortune in new lands. Or you may put your hand in Finn's hand and call him your captain. For I shall now give him his inheritance.'

Goll did not hesitate. He put his hand in Finn's hand and called him his captain. So did Caoilte, embracing Finn as if he were his own son.

Thus Finn MacCoull claimed his inheritance as Captain of the Fianna. He proved his worth to the people of Ireland that day, and gave them their first tale to tell of him.

While the news and celebrations spread, an old woman of the sidhe knelt over the headless body of her son on a high, cold, windy hilltop. Her keening was so loud that it was heard in the north and the south, the east and the west of the world, and no river ever ran so swift and deep as her tears.

BRAN & SCEOLAN

'Come out!' cried Finn.

The face of Teig, Muirne's father, appeared over his shining white ramparts. The old druid glared down at Finn, clutching his beard as it caught the wind.

'What do you want?'

'Justice,' said Finn. 'For my mother, whose own father turned her away when she carried a child inside her.'

'Arrogant whelp! You think that because you have the High King in your thrall, and a band of butchers at your command, you can challenge me!'

'I can. I do. Come out and face me, with words or weapons.'

Teig's mouth twisted into a snarl. He wanted nothing more than to summon druid-lightning and blast this brat into dust. But he knew about Finn; the tales had not spread slowly. His grandson had tasted the salmon of wisdom and defeated the fairy man of Sidhe Finnachaidh. Teig was a proud man; but he was a survivor.

'What can I offer you, if I will not fight you?' he asked.

'Your hall,' said Finn.

'My hall! You –' Teig stopped himself. He took a deep breath.

'It is done,' he said, his shoulders sagging in defeat.

✿

The fort on the Hill of Allen became the home of Finn and the Fianna. Finn sat in the chair where Teig had sat, and the Fianna

✿

came from across Ireland and Alba to meet their new captain and swear allegiance.

They found Finn to their liking. He was courteous to all, quick to laugh and quick to join in a game or wager. At feats of arms, none could best him, and he hunted well, though he had no hounds.

Young men poured in through the gates to take the tests. In order to join the Fianna, a man had to run through the forest without bending a blade of grass. He had to recite without error the twelve books of poetry; he would be buried in the earth up to his waist, and there defend himself against the swords of nine opponents, using nothing but a shield and hazel rod. Most men failed, but a few passed and became Fianna.

As for Finn? He woke in the morning and went to sleep smiling. To be surrounded by men of courage and wit; to hunt each day and feast by night; to fight in the practice yard or watch with his friends, joking and placing bets on the swordsmen; this was the best life a man could live.

He only wished that he had some hounds.

༼ᴥ༽

A band of Fianna from Ulster arrived at Allen one afternoon. Among them was a man named Iollan. Iollan bathed and dressed before sitting down with his brothers in the feasting hall, and as his eyes roved the hall, they alighted upon a woman at Finn's table.

'Who is that?' he asked his companion.

'That is Tuiren,' said the man. 'Finn's aunt. The woman beside her is Muirne, Finn's mother. She was living over the sea, and when she heard that Finn was Captain of the Fianna, she returned to Ireland and joined him here.'

'Tuiren,' said Iollan, who had barely heard another word after that one. 'What a lovely name. Tuiren,' he said again, enjoying its taste on his tongue.

༼ᴥ༽

Later that night, with mead-courage in him, Iollan spoke to Tuiren. They danced together, and the next day they took a walk in the forest together. Soon Iollan asked for a private audience with Finn.

'I wish to marry your aunt,' said Iollan, 'and return to Ulster with her. She loves me as I love her, and I will treat her well.'

Finn had seen that Iollan and Tuiren had taken to one another, and agreed to the marriage. 'Though,' he said, 'since I do not know you well, I will need more than your own assurances that you will treat her well.'

Iollan had expected this. He offered assurances from Goll, Caoilte and Lugaidh. Finn was satisfied, and the couple departed together.

Deep within the windy glens of Ulster was Iollan's home. It was no great hall, only a simple house, but Tuiren did not mind. Iollan hunted and fished to keep them fed, and Tuiren was kept busy doing the hundred things that needed done in a home each day. There were no neighbours nearby, but neither Iollan nor Tuiren minded much. They were content.

Winter came. The wind shrieked through the glen and the snow fell quickly and deeply. On a day when the sky was blue and clear, Iollan left for the market, leaving Tuiren alone in the snow-mantled house.

Tuiren sat by the fire, singing softly to herself as she prepared their supper.

There came a knock at the door.

Tuiren was surprised; they rarely received visitors. She stood, crossed the room and opened the door.

At first, she could do nothing but stare. Never in her life had she seen a woman as beautiful as the one who stood before her. She had hair like raven-feathers, pouting red lips and eyes that sparkled like dew on a spider's web at dawn. Her cloak was of thick fur taken from some animal unknown to Tuiren. The air around her seemed to softly sing, calling Tuiren out of her door, telling her to trust her visitor.

'My name is Uchtdealb,' said the stranger. 'Walk with me.' So Tuiren put on her cloak and stepped outside.

Through the snow they walked, taking a path that led into the forest. They passed beneath the sleeping trees, the crunch of their steps the only sound, until they came to a holly grove.

'It is cold,' said Tuiren, hugging herself. 'Perhaps we should go back.'

'Or we could stay here,' said Uchtdealb, 'among the hollies.'

She drew from within her cloak a wand of holly-bark.

'Are you a druid?' asked Tuiren.

Uchtdealb smiled. 'I am a sidhe,' she said. 'A Daughter of Danu. We are all druids, in our own way. As are you.'

'I am no druid,' said Tuiren.

'No?' asked Uchtdealb with a smile. 'But you have power.' She stepped closer to Tuiren. 'You made Iollan love you, as I could not. What greater power can anyone have than to capture the heart of their beloved?'

The mists in Tuiren's mind were clearing.

'I would like to go home now. Iollan will return soon, and he will miss me.'

Uchtdealb's smile became a sneer. 'I am sure he will, Tuiren. I am sure he will.'

The sidhe woman raised her wand and struck Tuiren. She screamed her spell, her forked tongue flickering in and out as strange lights shimmered among the holly trees and dark apparitions danced in the air.

Tuiren screamed and cried for Iollan. Uchtdealb laughed, licking Tuiren's face. She beat Tuiren with her wand until Tuiren fell to the forest floor, writhing and jerking as fur sprouted from her skin; her nose turned dark and wet; a tail grew from her rear and her cries turned to howls and barks.

'Come, Tuiren,' said Uchtdealb. 'There is someone I would like you to meet.'

❦

In another part of Ulster lived a hunter named Fergus. His house lay within a forest, and no visitors ever came to his door – although there had been a time when Uchtdealb would visit him.

Fergus was happy to be alone. He didn't care for company – although he had cared for Uchtdealb. So he was shocked to hear a knock on his door, and his heart sang when he saw her; until he saw the creature at her side.

'What is that … thing … doing here?' he asked. For while Fergus disliked people, he truly hated dogs.

'This,' said Uchtdealb, 'is Tuiren. Your new companion.'

'But –'

'Fergus,' said Uchtdealb. 'You are making me unhappy. You know what happens when you make me unhappy.'

Fergus trembled. 'Very well. Bring her inside.'

Uchtdealb knelt and stroked Tuiren. 'Go inside, my dear,' she said. 'Stay with this man. Run away and I shall know of it.'

Whimpering, Tuiren slunk past Fergus and into the house.

'Do as you wish with her,' said Uchtdealb to Fergus. 'Enjoy yourself. But keep her alive.'

That night, Fergus sat by his fire, watching Tuiren cower in the corner of the room.

'I could do anything I want with you,' he said.

Yet he knew Uchtdealb. There was more to this than she had told him. Much more. So he would leave the filthy creature alone.

For now.

❦

Morning came. Fergus dressed, took his bow from the wall and readied himself for the hunt.

'You won't be eating,' he said to Tuiren, 'unless you earn your meat.'

Fergus left the house and set off into the snowy forest, Tuiren at his side.

'Mark my words, hound,' he whispered. 'If you scare my prey off –'

Before he could finish his threat Tuiren surged forward, racing through the undergrowth. Moments later Fergus saw her leap upon the back of a fawn and bring it to the ground. It bleated in terror, then was silent.

Fergus ran to catch up.

'Well,' he said, panting as he stood over the fawn, its throat ripped out and Tuiren sat at its side. 'There's … there's a good girl. I suppose.'

He hoisted the fawn over his shoulder and went home to enjoy a day by the fire.

A few days later Tuiren proved her worth to Fergus once more. She did the same thing again and again, and Fergus began to realise that not only was it helpful to have a hunting hound, it was good to have a companion to sit with by the fire. He took to picking out the choicest cuts of meat for Tuiren, and he almost wished that he had a friend, so he could boast of her prowess. She loved to have her belly tickled; he loved waking up at night and hearing her breath, knowing he was not alone.

Before winter ended Fergus realised that Tuiren was pregnant. He stopped taking her hunting, leaving her by the fire instead. Many an evening he spent mulling over names for her pups.

❦

Fergus was happy.

Finn was not.

Word had reached his ears that Tuiren was not at Iollan's house. He sent messengers with an order for Iollan to come to Allen at once.

'Where is my aunt, Iollan?' asked Finn.

'Tuiren … she … she disappeared, one day when I was at market. I don't know where she went.'

'And you did not think to tell me?' said Finn.

'I was afraid. I did not know what you would do.'

'And you call yourself a man of the Fianna.'

Iollan hung his head.

'I am angry, Iollan. But I can forgive a mistake. I am giving you one chance to find my aunt. Fail to find her …'

'I'll find her,' said Iollan.

Iollan had a very good idea of what had happened to his wife. He knew well that Uchtdealb had never relinquished her love of him. Yet he was frightened of Uchtdealb. Was he more frightened of her than of Finn?

No, he realised on his long walk home. Finn would have his head if he did not deliver Tuiren; while Uchtdealb … he did not know what Uchtdealb would do with him. He never had; that was the attraction. Yet whatever she did, she would keep him alive.

Iollan did not go home. Instead, he turned east at the Ulster border, taking the road to the Mountains of Mourne.

Into the forested foothills he went. He found the trail he had once known so well, and followed it all the way to the wind-blasted peaks. Pulling his cloak tight about him, shivering in the icy mountain cold, he reached the doorway into the mountain.

Iollan spoke the words he had sworn he would never speak again.

The door opened. Uchtdealb smiled at him.

'The lost lamb returns,' she said.

'I have come for Tuiren,' said Iollan.

'You have come for me.'

'If she is alive, please give her to me, or Finn MacCoull will have my head.'

'And what will you give me, Iollan?'

'Whatever you want.'

'Very well,' said Uchtdealb. 'Go inside, my dear.'

With a last look around him, at a world he might never see again, Iollan passed the threshold into Uchtdealb's hall. Uchtdealb watched him walk down the hallway before stepping out onto the mountainside and sealing the door behind her.

Soon after that, she arrived at Fergus' house. Fergus called for her to enter, and she found him sat in his chair, two pups in his lap, while Tuiren lay stretched out before the fire.

'I am taking the hound back,' said Uchtdealb.

'But –'

Uchtdealb laughed. 'Do not tell me that Fergus has become a lover of hounds!'

'Well … I've got used to her, and …'

Fergus' pleading did him no good. Uchtdealb drew her wand and struck Tuiren with it.

Tuiren gave an unearthly howl. Fergus clutched the wriggling, yelping pups as their mother rolled on the floor, jerking and foaming, her eyes red and raw with pain. The fur fell from her, her tail receded into her and a few moments later she lay naked upon the floor, a woman again.

Fergus found a skin to cover her with.

'My children,' she said in a hoarse voice when she could finally speak. 'Turn my children too.'

'No,' said Uchtdealb. 'I think I would rather leave them as they are.' Laughing to herself, she left.

❦

❦

Tuiren left Fergus' house a few days later. He had asked her to stay; she refused with all the kindness she could muster.

With her pups at her side, she made her way south. There was only one place she could think to go. It was a long road, but in those days travellers could expect a warm welcome wherever they went. The days were cold, but each night saw her curled up at a fireside, her pups nestled in her arms. At last she stood before Finn in the hall of his fort, weeping as she told him her story.

'Stay here as long as you wish,' said Finn. 'Whatever you would have of me, you need only ask.'

'There is something.'

'Yes?'

'Take the pups. I cannot keep them.'

Finn eyed the pups, which were playing beneath the tables.

'Are you sure?'

'Yes. I love them, but …'

'I understand,' said Finn.

Tuiren left soon afterwards, returning to her father's hall. Finn did indeed keep the pups. He named the female Bran and the male Sceolan. Finn loved few people in his life more than he loved those hounds.

As for Iollan, he is probably still in Uchtdealb's hall, her lover and her prisoner.

THE LAD OF
THE SKINS

The air was sharp, the fire bright and the stars all awoken when the Lad of the Skins came prowling into Finn's camp.

Finn and his men were telling tales around the fire. The young man appeared out of the shadows, his short, muscular form adorned in the skins of wolves and men. Finn's companions leapt up, drew their swords and asked him his business, while Finn watched as Bran and Sceolan approached the Lad. They licked his hands and rubbed themselves against him. He stroked their fur, speaking to them in a strange tongue, before addressing himself to Finn.

'I am the Lad of the Skins,' he said, 'and I come seeking Finn MacCoull.'

'You have found him,' said Finn.

'I know,' said the Lad, 'and I ask to take service with you, whether it is for a long while or a short while.'

'I accept,' said Finn. 'Sit down with us.'

The Lad shook his head. 'I will return tomorrow,' he said, and melted into the shadows.

He appeared again in the morning, as the Fianna were rising and making ready for the hunt.

'On the hunt today,' he said to Finn, 'let us divide up the country. You and your men take the rich hunting grounds: the green woods and the flower-bright meadows. I will go meanwhile to the bogs and the high moors, and at day's end we will see whose hunting was more fruitful.'

Finn's bright blue eyes looked into those of the Lad.

'I agree,' said Finn.

He had the word put out among the Fianna and soon they and the Lad set off. The day brightened and darkened, and when the Fianna returned to camp that evening, they found the Lad sat atop a mountain of slain beasts. The Fianna, on the other hand, had managed only a few pigeons.

'Not to worry,' said the Lad with a smile, 'I will share what I caught.'

Some men were grateful, and set to skinning the meat. Others took it as an insult. One of these was Conan, who found Finn by the fire that night.

'You like this boy, don't you?' asked the bald warrior.

'I do,' said Finn, 'and I think that you don't.'

'I think he likes himself well enough for the both of us,' said Conan.

'So what would you ask?' said Finn.

'I would ask that he proves himself to be as fine as he thinks he is,' said Conan. 'By going to the hall of the King of the Floods and taking his Cauldron of Plenty. If he can do that, and bring it back here, I will like him twice as well as he likes himself.'

The Fianna feasted on a mountain of flesh that evening. The next morning, as they slept with full stomachs, the Lad came into the camp again. Finn was waiting for him.

'The King of the Floods,' said the Lad. 'I have heard of him, and his hall on an island far out to sea. I would be happy to go there, Finn, and to bring you back the Cauldron of Plenty.'

'I thought you would be,' said Finn.

The Lad turned and ran. He went west across the plain until he came to the hills, and when he reached them, he leapt from one hilltop to the next, all the way to the coast.

When he reached the beach, the Lad scoured the sands until he found two sticks of the same length. He rubbed them together, holding them up to the setting sun and speaking druid-words; then he tossed them onto the sand. The two sticks became many, and the Lad watched, laughing with delight, as they arranged themselves into a white-sailed ship. He gave the ship a great shove, leapt aboard and steered it out onto the ocean.

Far out on the whale-road he took his ship, past lands lost to legend and cities long sunken. After a short time or a long time, he spied spires in the blue sky, and at this sight he raised his fist and cheered. He had come to the hall of the King of the Floods.

The King's high hall came into view, perched atop a towering pinnacle of rock. A single winding stair ran up the pinnacle. At its foot was a harbour, and docked at the harbour was the greatest fleet of ships the Lad had ever seen.

He brought his ship up beside the nearest ship. Quickly furling her sails, the Lad drew his twin knives from their sheaths.

He bounded from ship to ship, and from ship to shore. He took the snaking path all the way to the King's hall at the top, and only once he stood at its doors did he stop to draw breath. The ships below him were tiny dots.

The doors of the hall were open.

The Lad entered the hall.

The King of the Floods was holding a feast. In attendance were the King of the Storms, the Queen of the Dead and the Father of Sickness; there were Fomorians too, and cat-headed men, dog-headed men and seal-folk. A ceiling of blue glass towered above them. The music was heartbreaking, joyous and wondrous, and the colours worn there were colours the Lad had not seen before.

He stood by the door, watching as folk talked, laughed, drank and danced. No one looked at him.

The Lad clapped his hands.

So loudly did he clap them that the music ceased. All eyes turned his way as he walked forward to stand before the throne of the King.

The King of the Floods was immense. He wore whale-skins and a necklace of whale-skulls, and the spear at his side was thicker than an oak tree.

'Some hall this is!' said the Lad. 'And some feast. I have been standing by the door, hungry and thirsty, and not a one here has offered me food or drink.'

The worth of a man was measured in those days by his generosity to guests. The King of the Floods was no different.

'Then you shall be given refreshment now,' he said in a bone-rattling voice. 'Pass to this young man the Cauldron.' And the Cauldron of Plenty was passed to the Lad.

He was offered a bowl. He took it, dipped it in the Cauldron, put it to his mouth and tipped back his head.

The Lad swallowed. He wiped his lips.

Grabbing the handles of the Cauldron, he turned and ran.

The Lad ran out the door and down the snaking road as the King's guests came howling and roaring after him. Many of them were swift, but none were as swift as him. The Lad reached the harbour and leapt from mast to mast, all the way to his ship. He took a set of oars in hand and rowed his ship east, away from the island. Each stroke he took covered leagues, and the Lad laughed as he sped over the sea.

He stopped rowing. His laughter ceased.

'What feat is it,' he asked himself, 'to take the cauldron running? It is a man who has never seen feats, who calls that a feat.'

So the Lad turned his ship around and returned to the island, where the feasters were still gathered at the harbour, cursing his name.

'There he is!' shouted one of the Dog-Heads.

A war-cry went up among the feasters.

〜❧〜

The Lad grinned, and unsheathed his knives.

Hours later he sheathed them again. The guests were all dead, the sea was strewn with their corpses, and the Lad's skins were red with blood.

'Time to take the Cauldron of Plenty to Finn,' he said to himself, and sailed away in his ship.

Far above, from the doorway of his hall, the King of the Floods watched the Lad sail away.

ꙮ

The Lad of the Skins brought the Cauldron to Finn. A feast was held in his honour at Allen and the bards set to work on telling his tale. He served with Finn for a time then left, with Finn's thanks and blessing, for he had been a good servant. Finn kept the Cauldron, and it gave him the plenty that it was named for, until one day it spoke.

'The King of the Floods is coming,' it said. 'He has raised an army, and they shall set sail soon, and if they reach Ireland you will not survive them.'

Finn touched his thumb to his tooth. It told him that the words of the Cauldron were true. Losing no time, Finn left the Hill of Allen, carrying the Cauldron, to seek out the Lad of the Skins.

He was spearfishing when Finn found him, beneath a hazel tree on a bend in the River Shannon. They greeted one another, and Finn told the Lad why he had come.

'I would surely help return the Cauldron to the King of the Floods,' said the Lad. 'But I am no longer your servant, and I cannot undertake any task for a man I do not serve. That is my wife's will.'

Finn was sorry to hear this, and surprised too, for the Lad had never mentioned his wife.

'Do not be vexed,' said the Lad. 'There is a way around this.

ꙮ

'My wife is Cliodhna, daughter of Manannan, Lord of the Sea. She lives with me in a tent near here, and every night she sings while combing her hair with a golden comb her father gave her. It is the way things are, that she cannot refuse any request made of her while she is combing her hair.'

Finn was glad to hear this, and he and the Lad spent the rest of the day fishing together.

That night, Finn stepped softly through the moonlit forest, listening for the song of Cliodhna. He heard it, and stopped to listen, for it was more beautiful than any singing he had ever heard. It made him think of leaping dolphins, silvery fish and dancers in cities deep beneath the waves.

Finn drew closer to the tent. It was made of willow branches and animal skins. Cliodhna went on singing, and Finn knelt outside until she paused in her song; then he spoke.

'I, Finn MacCoull, sit outside your tent. I ask you that your husband accompany me to the hall of the King of the Floods, to return the Cauldron of Plenty that was taken from him.'

The tent was silent.

'Very well,' said Cliodhna at last. 'But I shall ask something of you too, Finn. I ask that you bring my husband back to me, be he alive or dead. I shall wait on the shore for your return. If he returns alive, raise a grey-green sail. If he is dead, raise a red sail.'

Finn agreed. In the morning, he and the Lad departed.

They made their way to the coast, where the Lad again made a ship from sticks. The Lad wove a grey-green sail from grass and attached it to the mast. He made a red sail too, from fox furs, and stowed it on deck.

Over the waves they went. Finn wondered at the strange sights they saw, while the Lad captained them, for his sea-craft was best. Too soon they sighted the spire of the hall of the King of the Floods.

Their approach did not go unnoticed.

An army trooped out of the hall and down the path to the harbour. The King of the Floods watched from above.

Finn and the Lad leapt from ship to ship. They reached the harbour, where Finn drew his sword, as the Lad unsheathed his knives.

The army reached the foot of the path. Swinging their swords, hurling their spears, they charged at Finn and the Lad. Soon the pair were back-to-back, fighting with fury and delight as the hill of corpses beneath them grew. Night came, then morning, and it was as the sun sank again that they finally wiped their blades clean, their death-dance done.

Up the path they went with the Cauldron, and at the top they met the King.

'Thank you,' he said, 'and not just for returning my Cauldron. That was one of the finest fights I ever saw.'

Finn and the Lad were invited inside. They ate and drank and told stories with the King, and washed the blood from Finn's clothes and the Lad's skins. When they were ready to leave, and the Lad had collected some new skins to wear, they went east again, promising to visit. They sang and laughed as they made their way home across the sun-blessed blue ocean.

Finn and the Lad were not far from Ireland when a ship appeared on the horizon. Watching it draw closer, the Lad frowned.

'I know that ship,' he said. 'It belongs to a man who envies me, for my wife spurned his love.'

Finn watched the Lad as the ship approached. It was the first time he had seen his friend look afraid.

Soon the ship drew abreast with theirs. The man who steered it faced them from its deck. Suffering and hatred swam in his eyes.

'I told you that I would find you,' he said to the Lad. 'This time shall be the last.'

They leapt at one another, crashing down on the spurned man's deck. Finn could only watch as the Lad struggled; it was not a fight to join. The two were closely matched, and fought in near-silence, having no strength to spare for battle-cries. Waves slapped the two keels, the sun shone down and blood soon made the decks slippery.

So furiously did they fight that their fighting aged them. The Lad became a man, then an old man, and so did his adversary. When afternoon came they were clawing at one another with blue-veined fingers, until at last they fell together, without the strength to rise up.

At this time, their shape shifted again. They became puppies, nipping one another as they tumbled, and soon they were hounds, slavering as they tore fur and flesh from one another. As hounds they aged too, until they fell down together. They rose as foals and grew into stallions, lashing out with bone-breaking hooves.

Again they fell; again they rose up. This time they were eagles. Feathers flew as talons pierced flesh until, come the day's last light, the Lad's enemy fell down and did not rise up.

The Lad fell with him.

Finn rushed to the Lad's side, sank to his knees and cradled the Lad in his arms. As an eagle the Lad of the Skins fell, and as an eagle death took him.

All night Finn cradled the Lad in his arms, stretched near to breaking on the rack of sorrow. Yet Cliodhna was waiting, and when the half-light came Finn made himself stand. He spread his cloak on the deck, laid the Lad upon it and raised the red fox-fur sail.

He guided the ship back to Ireland. Green hills came into view, then dunes, then sand, and the Lad's wife stood upon the sand.

Finn gave Cliodhna the eagle that had been her husband. She held it in her arms, kissed his brow and bathed him in tears.

Bidding Finn goodbye, she made herself a ship as the Lad had made his. She laid the Lad out on the deck, pushed out her ship and sailed west.

Singing songs that the Lad had loved, she sailed far beyond the world.

Beyond dreams and imaginings she went, until one day she saw two great birds fly overhead, carrying another bird between them. She steered a course after them, and they led her to an island.

The island was mantled with forests and many-coloured mists. At its centre was a hill, and at the peak of the hill was a giant tree wreathed with clouds. She watched as the birds flew to its base, and watched them fly away again. The bird they had carried flew away with them.

Cliodhna rowed her ship to the island's shore. Cradling the Lad in her arms, she carried him, still an eagle, through the mist-wreathed forests of the island, all the way to the hill of the tree. She walked and climbed among its enormous roots until she reached the prow of the hill.

There, Cliodhna kissed the Lad again, and set him down at the foot of the tree. Seeing leaves scattered here and there, she gathered some and laid them upon her husband, until he was buried among them.

Cliodhna sat there, praying and singing through the days and nights, until there was a stirring among the leaves. She laughed and wept as her husband rose up, smiled at her and kissed her.

The Lad and Cliodhna stayed on the island awhile before returning to Ireland. They went to see Finn, who was overjoyed, and asked that the Lad take a place among the Fianna. But the Lad refused, and went away with his wife, and was never seen by Finn again.

THE BIRTH OF DIARMUID

Among the Fianna in the time of these tales was a man named Donn, son of Duibhne. He was well-known for being skilled with his sword, quick with his jests and handsome of face; but some said that he was cruel, and proud, and did not deserve a place among the Fianna.

Donn was feasting at Tara one winter night when he met a woman named Crochnuit. She had green eyes, dark curls and a quiet, elegant way about her. Donn was captivated, and cast a net of charm to ensnare her. Crochnuit seemed disinterested at first, but Donn persisted, plying her with mead and honeyed words until she relented. They kissed, and left the feasting hall together.

Soon the festival of Beltane came. It was a time when many couples chose to marry, and Donn and Crochnuit were among them that year. At sunrise they stood before a druid, speaking pledges of love and laughing as they fastened their hands together. They made a home and spent a joyful summer in one another's arms, seeing little of the sun. But come the winter months, when the fires of their passion began to fade, Crochnuit began to see Donn more clearly. She noticed the sharpness of his jests and the cold way in which he spoke to the poor. He shut their door on shivering travellers without offering food or drink; he spent nights away from home and would not say where he had slept.

The seasons turned and Beltane came again. In those days newly married couples would choose, after one year, whether to renew their bonds or part ways. Crochnuit couldn't wait to be parted from Donn, who didn't mind much; he had long since grown tired of her.

Crochnuit returned to her father's house. She did not return alone. Growing inside her was Donn's child.

Crochnuit gave birth to a boy and named him Diarmuid. Donn came to visit his son, but not often. Crochnuit raised Diarmuid, who bore her green eyes and dark curls, and she prayed that he would take after her in nature too.

It was the custom for teenage boys to be fostered with friends of the family or uncles. This time at last approached for Diarmuid, and Crochnuit's mind turned to finding a good foster home. She was distantly related to Finn, and she used her advantage in the way that people always have.

Crochnuit brought her boy to the Hill of Allen. They stood before Finn, and when Finn looked at Diarmuid, he saw something in the quiet, polite boy's green eyes. This boy, he thought, would be no ordinary man.

Finn found a place for Diarmuid; but not among the Fianna. Not with a lord, and not with a king.

Finn found Diarmuid a place in the halls of a god.

The Tuatha De Danaan, or Children of Danu, lived in Ireland before the Gaels came and drove them underground. Beneath the hills they built fabulous halls and there they dwell still, delighting in music, magic, fine food and poetry. Their lives are not bound by age like ours.

The Children of Danu are neither good nor bad; like us, they can be both. Yet some are greater than others, and some are so great as to be called gods.

One of these was Angus Og. Angus was the son of the All-Father, the mighty Dagda. His mother was Boinn, whom we call the River Boyne. Poetry and love were Angus' chief concerns and he had the gift of healing in his hands.

By a bend in the Boyne Angus had his hall, in the place where the great tomb of Newgrange stands today. Angus was fond of Finn, just as Finn was fond of Diarmuid, so when Finn asked Angus to foster Diarmuid, he gladly agreed.

Finn travelled with Diarmuid to the bend in the Boyne, and the door to Angus's hall was opened to them. Under the earth a sidhe man led them, through torch-lit passages decorated with carvings and jewels. Diarmuid could scarcely keep his mouth closed when he saw the hall itself; it was a mile wide and filled with thousands of feasting folk. Every person, every dish and every ornament he saw was more wondrous than the last, and the music played there would have made the stars weep.

Sat on his high throne was Angus Og, shining like the sun itself. He welcomed Finn and Diarmuid, and bade them sit beside him. Diarmuid was so dazzled by Angus that he was scared to approach him at first; but before long Angus had Diarmuid laughing, drinking and dancing as if he had lived in that hall all his life.

One year later, Crochnuit came to Finn's home again and asked to visit her son. Finn agreed. The two of them travelled to Angus' hall, and it was Crochnuit's turn to gape and gasp at its wonders. Yet no matter how dazzling the folk and the fare, it was the sight of her son, feasting at the side of Angus Og, that made her heart sing. She thanked Finn and Angus over and over again.

Later on, Crochnuit found herself conversing with a mortal man. He had fair hair, long limbs and kind eyes; he was a dazzling dancer and a druid too. He told her tales of the early days of the Tuatha De Danaan, and cast subtle spells so that she walked through the tales as he spoke. He asked her to dance, and they danced together as weeks passed in the world above.

Crochnuit did not want to leave. She stayed there, and married her fair-haired dancer, Roc Diocain, who served as Angus' steward. They had their wedding in Angus' hall, and Crochnuit was happier than she had ever dreamed possible.

Roc and Crochnuit had a son, whom they named Enda. Years passed, and again Crochnuit found herself thinking about fostering. Since Enda had grown up among the Tuatha De Danaan, she thought it would be good for him to know something of men; and there were no better men than the Fianna.

Roc travelled to the Hill of Allen. Finn was away, but Donn was there, and the two spoke in the feasting hall that night.

'I wish to foster my son here, among the Fianna,' said Roc. 'The mother of my child is the mother of your child, and it would give her great happiness if you could find a place for him.'

'Tell me,' said Donn. 'What is your rank in Angus' hall?'

'I am steward to Angus himself,' said Roc.

'Steward! You are a steward, and you think your son shall find a place here!' Donn roared with laughter, others turned to look and Roc's face reddened. He left the hall and took the road home that night.

Roc came home smarting and told Crochnuit there was no place for his son among those men. Thankfully, Angus heard about the debacle, and said that he himself would foster Enda. So Enda joined Diarmuid, his half-brother, at Angus' side.

The two boys grew up together. They learnt fighting and hunting, dancing and singing, poetry and tale-telling. Diarmuid was older than Enda, fiercely protective of him and keen to teach Enda all he knew.

❦

Diarmuid and Enda grew taller and stronger. They were fiercely loved by all in Angus' hall. Angus loved them as if they were his own sons, and gave them the best gifts he could find. He gifted Diarmuid a red spear and a yellow spear, and a sword of Manannan called the Great Fury.

One night, a company of Fianna led by Finn came to visit. Among them was Donn.

❦

As the musicians played and the dancers spun, Donn sat at his table, clutching his mead cup. His eyes were not on the fairy women; they followed Diarmuid and Enda as the pair moved through the hall, talking and joking with everyone they passed. His own son – Diarmuid, son of Donn of the Fianna – cavorting with the son of a lowly steward, one receiving no more respect than the other. It would not do. It was an insult.

Donn drank deeper, and refilled his cup.

Something had to be done.

A fight broke out among some of the hounds. More hounds joined, and more, and as folk ran to escape, Enda found himself caught amid the melee.

Enda ran – straight towards Donn.

Donn grabbed Enda, held him between his legs, and twisted Enda's neck until he felt it snap.

Enda fell lifeless to the floor. In the chaos no one noticed. But when the hounds ceased fighting, Enda's body was found and a cry went up. Roc came running. He fell to his knees and cradled Enda's lifeless body in his arms.

When the first flood of his grief had passed, Roc looked around him. All the feasters stood staring at him. His eyes found Finn.

'This is your fault!' he said. 'Your hounds killed my son. I will have the debt paid, here and now.'

❦

Finn studied the man and boy.

'You will,' he said. 'If you can find the mark of tooth or claw on him.' The steward searched, but could find no mark.

'Who did this?' screamed Roc. 'Who did this?'

Finn caught Angus' eye. 'Have one of your people bring me a bowl of water, a basin of gold and a gaming board,' he said.

This was done. Before the assembly, Finn spoke strange words to the water – words that he had learnt as a child from the druid Bodhmall.

The water glowed. Finn poured it in the basin, then dipped the gaming pieces in the basin. He moved the pieces on the board, singing softly to himself, and stopped.

Finn stood and turned towards Donn. His men had never seen him look so fearsome.

'Donn, son of Duibhne,' said Finn, 'is guilty.'

'It is quickly, then,' said Roc, 'that this debt shall be paid.'

Diarmuid was standing close to Roc, staring in shock at his friend's lifeless body. Roc seized Diarmuid and put Diarmuid's head between his own thighs.

Furious howls filled the hall. Donn made to approach Roc, as did Angus. Both held back – for Roc could snap Diarmuid's neck in an instant.

'Do this and you shall regret it,' said Angus.

Roc looked about him. He looked down at the trembling boy between his legs.

He released Diarmuid, threw him aside and rushed to the body of his own son. He knelt down and took from within his pockets a wand.

Roc spoke in the druid tongue. Into his words he poured his anger, his pain and all his power. The torchlight dimmed; phantoms danced through the dark air.

The steward raised his wand, sealed his spell and struck his son's corpse.

The boy twitched and shook. His skin peeled away and fell from his body. Like a snake Enda writhed and twisted before casting off his clothes and his skin, revealing a new shape beneath it.

Enda rose not as a boy but as a black-furred boar, dark intent glittering in its eyes.

The hall shook as the boar stamped its feet. It swung its tusks then turned and rushed away, up a tunnel and out of the hall.

'My boy, little Enda, was slain by the father of Diarmuid,' said Roc. 'Enda fell, and rose, and is now an animal. He shall dwell in cold, wild, rain-lashed places, while Diarmuid knows friendship, adventure and love. But these two, that were friends, shall meet again. When they do, the Black Boar shall be the death of Diarmuid.'

Diarmuid did grow up to know friendship, adventure and love, while the Black Boar dwelt in cold, wild, rain-lashed places. We shall hear more of Diarmuid, and of when he and the Black Boar finally met again.

THE GIANT'S
CAUSEWAY

On the north coast of Ireland lies one of the world's wonders. It is a road made of six-sided, interlocking basalt pillars, stretching from the foot of the towering cliffs of Antrim out into the sea, where it disappears from sight.

It is called the Giant's Causeway, and it was made by Finn MacCoull.

Finn was walking on the cliffs one day in spring. It was a fine morning and he was in a fine mood, for he was newly married and his wife, a beautiful red-haired woman named Oona, was pregnant with his child.

In a spot near Antrim's northernmost point, Finn stopped to put his hands on his hips and admire the view over to Alba. Finn was tall, and in those days men saw more clearly than they do now, so Finn was able to see all the way to the Island of Staffa.

Standing on the cliffs of Staffa was a giant.

The giant made a fine sight, outlined on the horizon, with the cliffs beneath him and the waves crashing beneath his feet. So Finn stood there awhile, enjoying the sight.

Only, that's not how the giant saw it.

His name was Benandonner. Of all the giants in Alba at that time, he was the biggest and cruellest. Other giants ran away or hid when they saw him coming, and he could smash holes in mountains with his bare fists. Yet as big and cruel as Benandonner was, he wasn't half as big or cruel as he was sensitive.

Benandonner hated being stared at. He saw Finn standing there on the Irish coast, watching him, and reasoned that Finn must be mocking him.

'Oi!' he shouted, his voice booming over the waves to Finn. 'What are you staring at, you –'

Benandonner called Finn a name so foul that all the milk in Ireland curdled as he spoke it. Finn answered in similar terms. Insults flew back and forth between them, growing more and more venomous, until they moved from insults to threats, and from threats to deeds.

Finn leapt from the clifftop down to the beach. He began to rip and pull at the bare rock, which broke apart into six-sided columns. These he arranged into what soon became a road, leading from the beach into the sea, towards Alba and towards Benandonner.

Over on Staffa, Benandonner began to do the same; then he changed his mind. Let Finn tire himself out, making a road to his own ruin.

Finn laboured and sweated day and night, going back and forth from the end of his road to the cliffs, adding column after column.

Benandonner watched and waited.

Several days later, Finn was halfway to Alba. He was tiring, but he was looking forward to reaching Alba and taking on Benandonner. This fight would make for a tale worth telling. But when he stopped for a break and looked towards Staffa, a jolt of fear ran through him.

Finn could see from where he stood that Benandonner was bigger than he had imagined.

Much, much bigger.

It wasn't in Finn's nature to run from a fight. But, he reasoned, this was different. He was utterly exhausted from building his road, and he knew he hadn't a chance against Benandonner. Besides, his wife was with child, he had responsibilities now …

Finn turned and ran.

He ran as fast as he could run; and as he went he heard a shout from behind him. Finn turned and saw Benandonner leap into the sea, surface and begin swimming after him. Panicking, Finn began tearing up his road as he went, so that Benandonner would not be able to chase him along it.

Finn reached the Irish shore. Leaving the last remnants of his ill-fated road in place, he ran for home.

Oona, Finn's wife, was stirring a pot over the fire when Finn came crashing in, panting and sweating and shouting. She was frightened, and even more frightened after Finn explained what had happened; but she was a good-minded woman. She took control of the situation.

'Here's what we're going to do,' she said. 'You are going to dress up as a baby. Then,' she said, before he could respond, 'you're going to get in there.' She pointed at the cot that Finn had been making for their unborn child.

Finn didn't like Oona's plan, but he couldn't think of a better one, and time was pressing. So he put on swaddling clothes and a frilly white cap, and climbed into the cot.

Oona covered him with a blanket and went back to the cooking pot.

The ground began to shake.

From outside the house, a voice as deep as the ocean called for Finn.

Oona went to the door.

Stood on the grass was Benandonner, red-bearded and angry-eyed, so huge that he blocked out the sun.

'Can I help you?' asked Oona.

'You are not Finn,' said Benandonner.

'That I'm not,' said Oona. 'I'm Finn's wife. Are you a friend of his?'

'Friend?' said Benandonner. 'Oh no, woman. I am anything but his friend. I am his doom.'

'Right then,' said Oona. 'Well, he's not in just now. He's out tending the goats. Come in and have an ale, he'll be back soon enough.'

'What? Oh … well … alright then,' said Benandonner, who, come to think of it, had quite a thirst. So, after enlarging the door, he entered and sat on the floor with his head pressed against the ceiling. Oona poured him an ale.

'How long will Finn be?' asked Benandonner.

'Not long,' said Oona, passing him their biggest drinking horn. 'Just relax and enjoy your ale. Where is it you're from, exactly?'

'Staffa. In Alba. You know it?'

So they passed the time as people do, until the ale was finished and Benandonner's anger overtook him.

'Enough of this!' he said. 'Either you take me to Finn now or I'll –'

'Wheesht!' said Oona. 'You'll wake the baby!'

At that, Benandonner's jaw dropped.

'Baby? Did you say … baby?'

'Yes. Our baby's sleeping over there, and you'll have me to answer to if you wake him.'

'A baby …' Benandonner turned and saw the cot at the far end of the house. 'A baby …' he said again.

Benandonner was fond of babies. He didn't like to eat them; he just liked them. Something about them softened his anger, and it was tiring to be angry all the time.

'Do you … do you think I could see him?'

'Of course,' said Oona, and they went over to the cot together.

'By my beard!' said Benandonner. 'He's enormous! He even has a beard himself!'

'Of course he does,' said Oona. 'What did you expect? He is Finn MacCoull's son, after all.'

'Oh … well, I suppose so,' said Benandonner, who was beginning to wonder if he had misjudged Finn's size. But no matter how big the baby was, it was still a baby. 'Do you think I might hold him?' he asked.

'If you're careful,' said Oona.

So Benandonner picked up Finn and cradled him in his arms. His face turned pink and he giggled as he said, 'Who's a good little lad? Who's a cutie-tooty?'

As he spoke, he stroked Finn's face with his giant fingers. When his little finger brushed Finn's mouth, Finn opened his eyes, opened his jaw and bit down on Benandonner's finger.

Benandonner screamed as Finn bit clean through his finger. To his credit, he didn't drop Finn, but placed him back in his cot before backing away towards the door, blood streaming from his finger.

'I'm so sorry,' said Oona. 'Let me see to that.'

'No,' said Benandonner, 'it's quite alright …' for he was thinking that if this was Finn's baby, he didn't want to meet Finn. He didn't want to meet Finn at all.

'I've just remembered,' he said, 'I've got something important to do back in Alba …' and he turned and ran.

Benandonner was never seen in Ireland again. But the remnants of his road still exist, in the sea by the island of Staffa, around Fingal's Cave. The remnants of Finn's road still mark the Antrim coast, and to stand upon them is to walk in the footsteps of Finn.

ᎯᏇᎨᎧ

BLACK, BROWN
& GREY

The peak of a mountain. The shores of the sea.

A deep cave, midsummer, midwinter.

These are places and times where worlds meet. And where worlds meet, there is often a gap that ill winds can slip through.

It was Samhain, the night on which the old year meets the new. After a summer of hunting and fighting, Finn and a band of Fianna had gathered at Finn's hall in Glen Lyon in Alba, where all winter long they would delight in feasting, song and story. The sun was setting, russet leaves were falling from the trees and men and their hounds were arriving. The men greeted one another, took horns of ale and gleefully awaited the start of the feasting.

Finn was pleased by this sight, but before the feast could start, he wanted to be sure that they were safe. He had not forgotten the fairy man of Sidhe Finnachaidh, who used to burn down the feasting hall at Tara each Samhain eve. So he called Bran to his side and went out to check that nothing strange was afoot in the woods.

Whispering winds stirred the last leaves as Finn and Bran passed through the autumn forest. Finn looked around, Bran sniffed the air and all seemed well to them. They were about to turn for home when they saw, standing on the far bank of a stream, three men.

The men crossed the stream and came to stand before Finn and Bran.

One of them was dressed entirely in black. He had black hair, black eyes, a black beard and he wore a black sword at his hip. The second of them was brown in all the ways the first one was black, and the third of them was grey in all the ways the second was brown.

'Greetings,' said Finn, and they returned his greeting. He asked them their names, and they gave them as Black, Brown and Grey.

'Why are you here?' asked Finn.

'We are here,' replied Black, 'because we heard you would be here. We are admirers of yours, Finn. After so many nights spent telling your tales around the fire, we decided to seek you out and ask if we might serve you.'

'You are generous,' said Finn, 'and as it happens, I have need of service tonight. The Fianna are gathered for a feast. Since tonight is Samhain, I would charge a few men with keeping watch. If you three would keep watch so that all my men may enjoy the feasting, I would consider it a great favour.'

'It is done,' said Black.

So Finn took his axe from his belt, chopped a nearby fallen log into three pieces and bade each of the men keep watch for as long as it took their log to burn.

'Bran will stay with you,' he said, and departed.

Black, Brown and Grey made their camp in that spot, and soon the sky was dark and Black's log was burning.

'I think I will go and have a look around,' said Black.

He made a torch from the flames of the fire, and as his companions set to cooking a meal, Black and Bran rose and went out into the dark woods.

They walked here and there through the glen, walking upon a thick carpet of fallen leaves. They saw nothing strange, and were about to turn back when Black saw pinpricks of firelight in the distance, as if there were a house that way.

'I have passed this way before,' he said to Bran, 'and I do not remember there being a house there.' So they went to investigate.

Soon they made out the shape of a hall. The doors were open and the sounds of feasting could be heard from within.

❧

Black and Bran entered the hall.

It was filled with beings from beyond the world. Cat-headed men conversed with wolf-headed men. Creatures with eyes in their stomachs danced with women who carried their hearts and brains in their hands. Tiny old men played by the fires while giant fat children nodded in chairs; and at the head of the gathering sat a two-headed, black-bearded giant.

Black stood in the doorway, taking it all in. He soon noticed that there was only a single cup to be seen among the company; and this he thought stranger than anything else.

The cup, he saw, was being passed around. Each reveller would take the cup and drink from it until it appeared to be drained, before passing it to another who would do the same.

Soon the cup came to Black. He looked within and saw that it was full. He drank. Whatever the liquid was, it was sweet. He emptied the cup and watched as it refilled itself, ready to be passed on.

Black looked around.

No one was watching him.

He looked at Bran. She seemed to understand his intent.

They turned and ran, hurtling through the woods all the way to their camp.

'Your turn, Brown,' said Black, appearing out of the shadows and giving his companion a kick.

Brown yawned, stood and wrapped his cloak about him. Taking a torch from the fire, he set off into the woods with Bran beside him.

Brown and Bran wandered through the woods of Glen Lyon. They saw nothing strange, and were about to turn back when Brown saw pinpricks of firelight in the distance, as if there were a house that way.

'I have been this way before,' he said to Bran, 'and I do not remember there being a house there.' So they went to investigate.

They came to the house, but Brown did not hear the sounds of feasting; he heard the sounds of fighting. Sword in hand, he approached the doors and peered in.

He saw the same strange company; but there was no celebration now. Everyone was shouting and pointing and every eye was wide with rage. A brawl seemed about to erupt when a gargantuan voice bellowed 'Stop!'

All fell silent.

Brown and Bran slipped inside as the two-headed, black-bearded giant rose and addressed the company.

'You dishonour my hall with your quarrelling,' the giant said.

'The cup is gone!' said a voice. 'We cannot feast without it!'

'That's because you took it!' said another voice.

'No, you took it!' called another.

'Stop!' said the giant again, his mouths moving as one. 'Whoever took the cup, we do not need it. I have something better.' He raised his fist, which held a knife. Before anyone could ask what was so special about it, he took a bone in his other hand and scraped the knife against the bone. As he did so, meat appeared on the bare bone and fell from there to his plate.

The feasters roared with delight. Musicians struck up, dancing began and the knife was passed around. Meat slammed down on the tables, and soon the knife came to Brown.

He gave Bran a look.

Bran knew what it meant.

They turned and ran.

༄

'Wake up, Grey! Time for your watch.'

Grey stirred himself from sleep as Brown made himself comfortable by the fire. Soon Grey and Bran were walking through the woods, Grey shivering under his cloak. They crossed the glen, and soon saw lights where Grey expected to see none.

'We'd best take a look at this, Bran,' said Grey. Bran whined, which surprised Grey, for Finn's favourite hound was said to be fearless.

They reached the hall. Firelight spilled through the doors; yet it was silent.

Grey and Bran stepped through the doors and looked around in horror.

The hall was full of corpses, torn and bloodied.

Grey walked the length of the hall, ignoring Bran's increasingly loud whines. At the end of the hall, he stopped and stared at the body of the two-headed giant.

༄

Bran's whined turned to yelping; then stopped.

As it stopped, Grey came to his senses. He looked into Bran's eyes and understood what she was telling him.

Something was coming.

A wind blew through the hall. Grey had never felt such a wind, but he knew what it was. It was a wind from the otherworld, blowing in through the crack between the worlds; and a being from a far, dark place rode upon it.

He heard a shuffling from the darkness outside the hall, and a sniffing.

Grey and Bran dropped to the ground. They buried themselves among the corpses and pretended to be dead.

Through unblinking eyes, Grey watched the visitor enter.

She was an old woman; as old as time itself. Her skin was blue and grey; her hair was matted cobwebs. She wore no clothes and had only one eye, one arm and one leg. A giant fang extended from her mouth to the ground, and she walked using her fang as a crutch.

Sniffing the air, she grinned. Slamming her fang into the floor, she moved forward, fell upon the first corpse and began to feed. Grey watched as she ripped and tore and guzzled on eye and tongue, heart and hamstring until not a bone remained of the cat-headed man she had dined on.

Fattened from her feast, the hag moved into the hall.

Onward she went, eating with a speed and appetite that seemed only to increase. Her stomach grew and bulged until she was the largest and fattest thing Grey had ever seen, and she had to drag herself across the floor to the next corpse, her fang sinking deep into the earthen floor. All the time, she was drawing closer to Grey and Bran.

She reached the corpses that covered them. She set to work, biting and tearing and crunching until Grey and Bran lay uncovered before her.

The old woman threw back her head. Her raised fang gleamed in the firelight.

Grey and Bran tensed themselves, ready to leap aside.

The old woman fell asleep.

She was so full that she could stay awake no longer. As Grey and Bran leapt away she collapsed, her fang thudding into the ground where Bran's head had lain a moment before. Grey and Bran ran from the house; but Grey stopped at the entrance and turned back.

'It is not my way to kill a sleeping enemy,' he said to Bran. 'But I will kill her.' So he walked back through the house and drew his grey sword. With a two-handed swing he sliced the old woman open from throat to stomach.

A torrent of foul fluid erupted from the wound, and three men leapt out from her chest. Each landed with a roar and with his sword drawn.

One was blue beneath the blood and bile. His clothes, his hair, his sword were blue. The second man was green, and the third was red.

The blue warrior roared again and charged at Grey. Grey recovered from his surprise, swung his sword and fought with the blue warrior, soon striking him down. Bran leapt at the green man, tearing out his throat, and when the red warrior saw this, he turned and ran. Grey let him go.

As the sun rose, Grey returned to camp. He and his companions made their breakfast and told their tales until Finn appeared.

'How passed the night?' asked Finn.

They told him how it had passed.

'This cup of plenty, I give to you,' said Black, after Grey had told the final part of the tale. He gave Finn the cup, and likewise Brown gave Finn the knife. Grey had nothing to give.

'I thank you all,' said Finn. 'And if you ever wish to take the trials to join us, I would be glad of it. I must say one thing, though.' He looked at Grey. 'I wish you hadn't let that red warrior run. I have a feeling that he and I will meet, and that I will be the worse for it.'

❧

So the three warriors accepted Finn's thanks and went on their way. Finn and Bran returned to Finn's hall, and the tale of Black, Brown and Grey was told many times that winter.

But so were other tales; and Finn met many red-haired men on his travels. So when, a few years later, a red-haired warrior came into his camp and asked to take the trials, he did not think anything of it. The man passed the trials, and was admitted to the Fianna.

'What wages would you have of me?' Finn asked the red-haired man.

'Only this,' said the red-haired man. 'That if, after twenty-one years, I have served you well, you come to a feast at my home.'

Finn agreed to that, and the man served him well for twenty-one years.

'Well, Finn,' he said. 'About that feast.'

So Finn travelled with the red-haired man through Alba. They came to Loch Lomond and travelled on a little boat to an island in the middle of the loch. Up a path lay the red-haired warrior's hall. Finn entered and saw that the feast was already laid out.

'Sit down, Finn,' said the red-haired warrior.

Finn sat.

'Try some of the mead in that jug, Finn,' said the red-haired warrior.

So Finn rose to reach for the jug; but he could not move from his chair.

The red-haired warrior laughed. 'At last, I have you.'

'You have me?' asked Finn.

'You don't recognise me, do you, Finn? Well, we never met, it is true. You have other men do your sword-work for you. You had Black, Brown and Grey stalk the forest that night, while you sat in your hall, filling your fair face. As the great Finn feasted, those men murdered my mother – my dear, sweet mother – and my brothers.

'But justice is mine this day. Finally, Finn, you shall die.' The red-haired warrior took a red sword down from the wall.

'Do you have a last request, Finn MacCoull?'

Finn thought for a moment.

'Yes,' he said. 'I would like to blow my horn, and enjoy its sweet song one last time.'

'Granted. Wait ... no, hold on –'

But it was too late. Finn had taken the Dord Fiann, the Horn of the Fianna, from his belt. He blew a mighty blast upon it, then tossed it aside and drew his sword as his enemy came at him.

Still stuck to his chair, Finn fought and held his opponent off; until the door crashed down, the Fianna poured in and the red-haired warrior was cut into pieces.

After that, Finn could stand again, but he didn't. He sat with his men and enjoyed the feast.

THE BIRTH
OF OSSIAN

It happened this way.

From the Hill of Allen, Finn set out one morning. His men ran beside him, their hounds raced ahead of them and the rising sun was bright at their back. They entered the green wood, startled a hind and cheered as they gave chase.

The hind kept ahead of them, and at noon it was still not theirs. The men wondered at its speed and guile, and as the afternoon wore on, some gave up and called off their hounds. Come the twilight, only Finn and his hounds remained.

Ahead of Finn, out of sight, Bran and Sceolan began to bark furiously. Finn smiled wearily, for he knew what that meant. The chase was over. Finn ran to catch up with his hounds. He entered the clearing where they awaited him, and saw something there that he had not seen before.

Bran and Sceolan had cornered the hind; yet they had not brought it down. It lay on the grass, gazing at Finn as they danced around it, nuzzling and licking it.

This was no ordinary deer. Finn savoured the presence of the otherworld, meeting the hind's gaze as the night embraced them.

It was time to turn for home. Finn called Bran and Sceolan to his side. They came, and so did the hind.

It followed them all the way to the Fort of the Fianna. Through the gates it walked. Soon word spread and folk came to watch as it wandered here and there, nibbling the grass in the torchlight, unafraid.

At length the Fianna gathered in the feasting hall, where Finn told the tale of the day. They ate and drank until they tired, then went their chambers. Before going to his chamber, Finn went out and found the hind. The two of them watched one another for a while before Finn turned and left.

He went to bed, and fell asleep.

୧୭୨

When Finn awoke, it was to the quiet of the deep night, the flickering light of his fire, and the sound of his door opening.

Finn sat up in his bed. He stared as a woman entered his chamber. The firelight danced upon her naked body, her auburn curls and her chestnut eyes, which never left his own. She won his heart before her first footstep fell.

Without speaking a word she climbed into his bed; he made room for her beside him. She nestled into his arms, and Finn found he had not the wit to say a word. So she smiled, and spoke to him.

'The deer that you chased through the green wood was me. I am Sabha. I was a woman as I am now, until the Dark Druid of the Tuatha De Danaan fell in love with me. He asked me to marry him, and to live with him in his underground hall, and I refused.

'He asked again, and I refused again, and so it went until he grew angry and used his magic against me. He struck me with his wand and made me into a hind.

'For three winters and three summers I wandered in that way. At last, a former servant of the Dark Druid sought me out. He told me that the day I met you, I would be released from the spell.'

Sabha kissed Finn. He returned her kiss, and no more words were spoken between them that night.

୧୭୨

୧୭୨

When Finn reappeared a few days later, it was with Sabha at his side. She sat beside him in the feasting hall, and he spoke only with her.

'Will you join us on the hunt tomorrow, Finn?' asked Caoilte.

'No,' said Finn, 'I will be with Sabha tomorrow, and the next day too.'

So it went as it always does. Finn gave himself to Sabha, and she to him, and all his pursuits and passions were lost in the throes of their embrace. The Fianna were glad to see Finn happy, yet sad that he seemed to have forgotten them. They found themselves hunting less, for he would not join them, and in the practice yard less, for Finn never stopped by. By night they drank deeper, and told fewer tales.

It was in this time that the Fomorians came.

The Fomorians dwelt beneath the western sea and upon its rocky islands. Often they would send raiding parties to Ireland, and always the Fianna would defeat them. But this was no raiding party.

The Fomorian druids had divined a weakness in the Fianna. The druids told their Kings, who forged an alliance and raised an armada to strike at Ireland. From the dark isles of the west and the nightmare cities of the deep sea, there came such a force as had not been mustered since their first war with the Gaels. For league after league, their sails blackened the sea.

Finn's own druids were not idle. They caught the winds of magic that streamed ahead of the fleet. Beacons were lit, messengers took to the road and all the Fianna of Ireland made for the bay where the spear-tip would strike.

Almost all of the Fianna.

When the first man knocked on Finn's door, he did not answer. Finn shouted to the second man not to disturb him, and a dozen others had come and gone before finally he answered the door to Caoilte, dressed in a way that said that important business was being interrupted.

'Ireland is under attack,' said Caoilte.

'There are a thousand Fianna and more,' said Finn. 'I am not needed.'

'If you are not needed, you are not our Captain,' said Caoilte.

'I am your Captain,' said Finn, 'and I am telling you to leave me in peace.'

'Your father would be ashamed of you,' said Caoilte.

Those were the hardest words Caoilte ever said to Finn. Finn looked set to strike Caoilte, but he stopped when saw himself reflected in his friend's eyes. Caoilte had been a friend of Coull, Finn's father. This was no idle insult. It was the truth.

Finn dressed and armed himself. He bid Sabha goodbye and ran with Caoilte, all the way to the hill overlooking the bay where the Fomorian army had come ashore and were fighting the Fianna.

Down the hill came Finn. He blew the Dord Fiann, the Horn of the Fianna, and his men cheered and fought twice as hard as before. He put away his horn and roared as he met the Fomorian forces.

So deadly was Finn's sword that many of his enemies dropped their weapons and ran into the sea. Those that stood and fought fell like leaves in autumn, and his own men kept back, as in his fury he knew not friend from foe. The Fomorians were so many that their footsteps shook their earth; yet they were helpless in the face of Finn's battle dance.

❦

For eight days and nights the battle raged. Heaps of dead became hills, became mountains; blood flowed in rivers, ravens growing fat as they gorged.

Finally it was over. The Fomorians were defeated. Those few who survived swam away; their boats were burned.

The Fianna spent a day making pyres of their own dead. That night they gathered on the beach, to light the torches and to drink and sing as their fallen brothers passed into the next world.

❦

As they drank, sang, keened and wept, they saw Finn preparing to depart. It was Caoilte again who went to him.

'You are not leaving,' said Caoilte.

'My duty is done. I have a wife who is waiting for me, and I will not be dissuaded.'

Caoilte did not speak further. He only looked at Finn. Finn saw that the old warrior was hurt with many wounds. He saw the light reflected in Caoilte's eyes, cast by fires on which their friends burned.

Finn was ashamed. He stayed, and remained on the beach all night, walking among his men and dispensing praise. Yet his eyes were ever on the wheeling of the stars.

Come morning he left. He ran for home and soon spied the Hill of Allen rising above the forest, his white fort shining in the morning light. Through the forest he ran and up the hill, calling Sabha's name. He looked for her as he ran to the gate, expecting to see her appear, but she did not.

Finn slowed as the serving folk gathered at the gate to greet him. None would meet his gaze.

Finn stopped before them.

'Where is Sabha?' he asked.

An old man stepped forward. He met Finn's eyes, and his own eyes were full of grief.

'Every day since you left,' said the man, 'she would stand atop the wall, watching for your return.

'Three days ago, we heard her cry out with joy, and we knew she had seen you coming. I went up to join her on the wall, for I looked forward to your return too. There you were indeed, and she was all set to go out to you; but I had an ill feeling, and I bade her stay. But she wouldn't listen,' said the old man, shaking his head. 'She said to me, "How can I not go out and greet my husband, the … the father of my child."

'So she went to you, and I saw her put her arms around you, out on the path there. But the moment she did, the one that she thought was you, he changed. His face was different; he wore a druid's robe. The druid spoke harsh words to her, and she to him; and then he struck her with a wand.'

'What happened then?' asked Finn.

'She … she became a deer. The moment she did, she tried to run, but he spoke a spell that made her turn and follow him into the wood. We went after them but could not find them.'

Finn spoke no words. He left his servants, went to his room and would see no one. Into dark dreams he fell and through wastelands of grief he wandered, staring empty-eyed into the ashes of his fire.

Days later, he arose from his chair. He went outside and called Bran and Sceolan to him. She had to be somewhere; and wherever that was, he and his hounds would find her.

They left the fort. It is said that for seven long years they searched for Sabha. It was hard for Bran and Sceolan to see Finn in such pain, and they pressed their bodies close to his as he wept in the forests and on the windy moors. Not a house in Ireland did they fail to search. There was not a blade of grass in any field, a rock upon any hillside that they did not step upon seven times. Yet they found no sign of her.

At long last, Finn turned for home. Though he still longed for Sabha, those years spent wandering his beloved homeland had eased his grief. He had sat atop mountains bathed in storm light; he had lingered in the deep forest's shadowy embrace. Finn remembered that his heart's love was too great to be solely for Sabha. It was for his brothers, his hounds and every stranger on the road; every raven, every foxhole and every freezing winter wind.

It was a happier Finn who joined the hunt one day, soon after his return.

Bran and Sceolan and the other hounds were ahead, lost to sight in the dense foliage. Finn heard barking and he and the other hunters ran towards the sound. They caught up with the hounds and once again, Finn saw something he had not seen before.

The hounds had not caught a deer.

They had caught a human child.

It was a naked boy, with long, fair hair and a wild look about him. The hounds seemed to think him a creature of the wild; they had encircled him and were growling and snapping their teeth. But Bran and Sceolan stood between the boy and the other hounds, keeping them back.

The boy laughed and smiled as he watched Bran and Sceolan. He seemed entirely unafraid.

'Call off your hounds,' said Finn to his men. They did so.

In the sudden quiet, Finn stepped forward and knelt down before the boy. The boy looked into Finn's eyes and smiled at him.

Finn smiled back. He knew those eyes. They were his own.

Finn picked up the boy and carried him home. He had clothes made for him, though the boy seemed unaccustomed to wearing any. Finn sat the boy on his lap at mealtimes, and the boy played with the knives, forks and spoons as if he had never seen such things. Finn asked him his name, and many questions, but the boy knew no Gaelic; only strange grunts and purrs.

The boy slept beside Finn, and went everywhere with him. Finn guarded him fiercely, and taught him everything he could teach him. He spoke to him all the time, about anything and everything. Soon enough, the boy began speaking too.

One night, sat on Finn's lap by his fire, he told Finn his story.

'My mother was a deer,' he said. 'We lived in a forest like the one in which you found me; but it was unlike it, for we could not escape. At its borders were cliff walls which my mother could not climb.

'In every other way, it was a good place. There were animals and birds to play and sing with, and streams to swim in and trees to climb. I was happy there, but my mother was not, because of the one who kept her there.'

'Tell me of him,' said Finn.

'I didn't like him,' said the boy. 'He never spoke much to me, but he scared my mother when he came to visit. Sometimes he would speak softly to her, as if he cared for her. At other times he sounded harsh and angry; I didn't understand his words. I could see, though, that he wanted something from her, and that she refused him; until one day he took a wand from the folds of his cloak and struck her with it.'

A tear rolled down the boy's cheek. Finn stroked his hair.

'He put his wand away, then turned and walked off, gesturing for my mother to follow him. She did. I could see that she didn't want to, and she turned and cried out to me as she went, but she went.

'I followed, but I am small, and I couldn't keep up with them. They disappeared, and I couldn't find them. I cried for my mother, and I think I must have fallen asleep. When I woke up, I was in the forest where you found me.'

Thus Finn finally learnt the truth that his heart already knew. The boy was his son. As fierce and all-consuming as his love for Sabha had been, it was like a raindrop compared to the ocean of love he felt for the boy. Finn told the boy that he was his father, and that he would protect him as the boy's mother had done.

Finn gave the boy a name. He called him Ossian, which means Little Deer.

PART II

THE HIGH DAYS OF FINN

DARK, BATTLE & EAGLE

The Fianna loved to tell tales of the trials they had faced, of battles won, their brothers slain in noble combat. But there were some stories they refused to tell, some memories they would not revisit. Such was the tale of Dark, Battle and Eagle.

A band of Fianna led by Finn made a hunting camp in the forests of Alba one summer. They hunted by day and gathered by blazing fires each night, telling tales of the hunt and of battles gone by, or singing along to the songs of their bards. The hunting was good, the company was better and the life was all that any Fianna could ask for.

One day, three men arrived in their camp at dawn. Word went out quickly and all the Fianna rose and came to see them, for these were clearly no ordinary men.

They gave their names to Finn as Dark, Battle and Eagle. With them they had a hound that glittered with all the colours of the rainbow.

'What do you want with us?' asked Finn.

'We wish to take service,' said Dark.

'And what can you offer us?' asked Finn.

'I can offer you peace, as the day ends and the fire beckons,' said Dark. 'For I can do the watching for all of your men.'

'I can offer you a guarantee of good hunting,' said Battle. 'For our hound will bring down a deer every second day, if not better.'

'I can offer you rest,' said Eagle. 'For I have a pipe that will send every man of the Fianna into peaceful sleep.'

There was muttering among the Fianna then, for these men unsettled them. If Dark, Battle and Eagle could do all they claimed, then they were powerful; should such men be trusted? But Finn said to them, 'You may take service with us. Go make your camp.'

'We have a condition of our own,' said Battle. More muttering; who would ask to take service with Finn, and then make demands? 'We will make our own camp, and we need assurance that none will come near it at night.'

'Why is that?' asked Finn.

'Because each of us is dead, every third night,' answered Eagle. 'And we don't like to be seen when we are that way.'

To this Finn agreed. They made their camp, and set about it a wall of fire.

Days and nights passed, the sun and moon spun and Dark, Battle and Eagle lived up to their promises. When the hunting went ill, their glittering hound brought down deer that even Bran and Sceolan could not catch. Meat filled the bellies of the hunters and they found themselves thinking better of their new companions. When storms wracked the camp and rain soaked their tents, Dark kept watch while Eagle's pipe pulled them into blissful sleep. These men were strange, yes; but so were many things in the world, and life was good.

Those days of peace in the glens of Alba soon passed.

༺༻

It was night-time. The last men standing had gathered at Finn's fire, drunk and merry, clutching their cups. Dark, Battle and Eagle were encased in their ring of flame. Caoilte was midway through a tale when the hounds sprang up, barking furiously at the darkness.

Into the firelight came three fiends.

They were men, but not men. Clad in red rags, they moved like beasts, leaping and crawling, laughing and weeping at once. The

༺༻

tears they wept were blood, and a foul-smelling liquid, that was surely poison, dripped from their eyes and mouths, their hands and feet.

Finn came forward as the other Fianna backed away.

'You have entered our camp unbidden,' he said. 'Who are you and what do you want with the Fianna?'

'We are Ill-Wishing, Harm and Want,' said the first of them, whom Finn took to be Ill-Wishing. 'And we are here to collect payment.'

'For what debt?' asked Finn.

'For the death of our father,' said Harm, looking at Caoilte. 'For this one slew Uar, our father, in battle.'

'Then be gone with you,' said Finn. 'No blood price was ever collected for a man slain in battle.'

'Then this shall be the first time,' said Want.

'What if it isn't?' asked Caoilte.

At that the three fiends laughed. Blood and poison poured from them.

'Then we will take your feet,' said Ill-Wishing. The others rolled on the ground, shrieking and whooping at his words. 'And your hands. We will take your hounds, and your serving boys, and gouge out their eyes.'

Finn drew his sword, each Fianna drew his own and with a roar they ran forward; but the Sons of Uar vanished like smoke. The only proof that they had been there was the blood and poison-soaked earth.

'A fear is upon me,' said Caoilte. 'I fear that those foul creatures will be the end of the Fianna.'

No man slept well in the camp that night. Nightmares plagued the warriors. Finn and Caoilte and the other leaders talked through the dark hours, and when the men rose bleary-eyed in the morning, they learnt that there would be no hunt that day. Dark, Battle, Eagle and their shimmering hound would hunt. The rest of them were to build earthen walls about the camp. Guards would be posted about the walls, night and day, to watch for the Sons of Uar.

This was done. The rainbow hound brought home a deer, and its meat was roasted that night. There was no talk beside the fire. The Fianna were afraid, and it shamed and disturbed them equally.

They could not and would not remain in camp, though. There was foraging to be done, there was water to be collected; and a distrust of Dark, Battle and Eagle was in the air again. After all, had they not arrived at around the same time as the Sons of Uar? What if the deer their hound brought down was ill-fated?

Finn spoke against this but suspicion had taken root. Men began to desert camp, and it was not the way of Finn to stop them.

They returned to camp crawling on bloody stumps. Their eyeless hounds and serving boys were tossed, howling, over the walls. The Sons of Uar came and went like phantoms in the night.

The Fianna would not abandon their camp; nor, it seemed, could they. They were under siege. Were it not for Dark, Battle and Eagle, they would have starved. Yet still the warriors could not trust such men, who died and rose again behind a wall of flame.

So the days and months and seasons passed. The Fianna grew ever thinner, weaker, more sorrowful; they wept to see bones poking out through the fur of their hounds. Some even fought one another, and now and then a man would attempt to escape. They came crawling back, eyeless, or died in the hands of their enemies, their hands and feet thrown over the earthen walls.

It seemed that Caoilte's prophecy would come true. The last days of the Fianna were upon them.

One dark winter morning, the blast of horns rang through the forest.

Shivering men emerged from their tents. Hands went to sword hilts as the horns went on blowing.

❦

Had their enemies come to end the feud? Some welcomed the thought of spilling hot blood on the snow, even were it their own. Either way, the horror would be over.

But this was not the Sons of Uar.

Finn climbed the wall by the gate and saw the King of Alba riding towards him. The two warriors had feasted together and knew one another well. Finn laughed, called out a welcome to the King and opened the gates.

Fresh logs were thrown on the fires; meat and drink were given to their visitors. The King and his men ate and drank while listening with grim faces to Finn's tale.

Once Finn had finished, the King thought for a while, then spoke.

'It pains me to hear what you have suffered. It pains me more to think that you may have suffered in vain. For these men that you speak of, that have kept you fed and tended to your wounds; they must be gifted druids. Why have you not asked their help in ridding yourselves of these ghouls?'

Finn looked at his men, who averted their eyes. Many times he had wished to enlist further help from Dark, Battle and Eagle; but all his men had argued against it.

He realised then that he should have looked to his own judgement, if he was any captain at all.

'Would you speak with them?' asked Finn.

'I would,' said the King. So they were sent for, and when they arrived the King asked if they could banish the Sons of Uar.

'If they are brought before us, we can try,' said Battle.

'Go out into the woods,' said the King. He pointed to two of Finn's men, Lugaidh and Garb-Cronan. 'Call out the Sons of Uar, and tell them Finn MacCoull wishes to recompense them.'

So Lugaidh and Garb-Cronan departed, and it was not long before they came back into the camp, bringing with them Ill-Wishing, Harm and Want. They leered and danced as poison dripped from them, hissing as it met the snow.

'You have decided to pay the blood price,' said Want.

Dark, Battle and Eagle stepped forward. Their rainbow-coloured hound was beside them.

The Sons of Uar stopped their grinning and leaping. They snarled, spat and bared their teeth. Hope sprang up among the Fianna, for their enemies looked afraid.

'A blood price shall be paid,' said Finn.

Before their enemies could answer, Dark began to chant.

He spoke druid words that none there understood, yet all felt their power. The air crackled; a wind rose up and swirled through the camp; and as Dark reached his crescendo, the hound opened its jaws.

It sucked in the wind and blew it back out, with ten times more power. The wind struck the Sons of Uar. They were tossed, shrieking, into the air and flew away over the treetops. Though the Fianna could not see it, they were blown all the way over the mountains of Alba, even over the mighty Seat of the Hag, and only released when they were far out to sea. They hit the water and drowned, pulling one another into the depths.

So the siege ended. The King sent for provisions, and when they came a feast was held. The Fianna rebuilt their strength and mourned their dead. Dark, Battle and Eagle were no longer shunned, but honoured. The Fianna remained at camp, as midwinter came and the days began to lengthen.

One day, a serving man of the King's heard the tale of how those druids became corpses, and wished to see for himself. He approached their camp one night in secret, and peered through the wall of flames that encircled it.

He saw Eagle, lying dead. He saw that their hound had become a tiny creature, a pup that might have fit in his hand. Dark held a cup to its lips, and from its lips would pour ale, mead or whatever drink Dark asked of it.

'Take note,' said Battle, 'of the treachery done to us.' He turned to look at the watcher.

The hound growled and grew to its former size. It leapt through the flames, seized the serving man and dragged him into the fire circle. There Dark and Battle killed and butchered him, and he was eaten by the hound.

Dark, Battle and Eagle were gone the next morning. They were not seen again.

FINN & THE FOOL

It was many years after Sabha was stolen when Finn finally took a wife again.

Her name was Lorna, of the Luigne people of Ulster. Finn was feasting in Ulster when he met her, and like most men who looked upon her, he could not look away. She was the finest dancer in Ireland, her singing was as gentle and as fierce as the tides and her eyes promised nights with not a thought of sleep. Lorna danced with Finn, pressed her body close to his and he was hers.

They fastened their hands together soon afterwards. Finn made a house for them in Ulster, for Lorna said she could not bear to leave the hills and glens of the north. Finn believed her.

At the same feast where Finn met Lorna, he saw a fool performing. This fool juggled fire, sang nonsense songs and mocked everyone – even Finn. Finn took a liking to him. He brought the fool home to live a season or two in his house, for he missed the companionship of the Fianna, especially Diarmuid and Ossian. Diarmuid had grown into a fine warrior and an even finer friend, while Ossian was a fearsome fighter, the greatest of poets and the pride of Finn's heart.

Finn and the fool got on famously. Finn loved the fool's stories, his playing and his mockery – for no one else ever dared mock Finn. But Lorna wasn't so keen.

Lorna didn't like being mocked. What she disliked even more was having the fool around the house while Finn was away hunting. For Lorna liked to use those times to entertain guests.

There was one guest whom she entertained as often as possible. His name was Coirpre. He was a lord of the Luigne people, handsome and proud. Coirpre loved the thought of humiliating the oh-so-mighty Finn MacCoull by having his way with Finn's wife. So Coirpre often came to visit and take Lorna in Finn's bed, after Lorna had sent the fool out on some errand.

'Fool, we need more firewood,' she'd say. 'You're looking pale, Fool, why don't you take a long walk in the sunshine?'

Of course, this couldn't go on forever. One day the fool came home with a black rabbit for Lorna to make gloves from, just as she had asked, to find Coirpre and Lorna naked on the floor together.

Lorna saw him and shrieked. Coirpre saw him, got to his feet, wrapped a fur around his waist and walked over to the fool.

'You listen here,' he said, wrapping his fingers around the fool's throat. 'If Finn hears a word of this, I'll cut out your tongue and shove it where no one will ever find it.'

'Flibby-wibby,' said the fool with a sad, slow nod.

Coirpre dressed and left.

The fool avoided Finn's eyes that evening. He feigned a stomach ache and went to bed early. He didn't sleep. The fool loved Finn, and in his mind, by not telling Finn, he was as good as betraying Finn himself. But he was afraid of Coirpre. He didn't want his tongue cut off or shoved anywhere. So he kept quiet.

The fool couldn't bear it. He could hardly look at Finn, let alone make a good jest for him. So he took to walking alone in the woods from dawn to dusk.

'I think something is upsetting the fool,' Finn said to Lorna.

'He's always been soft in the head,' said Lorna. 'That's why he's a fool, and why you keep him.'

Days and weeks passed. The fool grew more and more unhappy; and then, sitting on a log in the forest one day, he had an idea.

' *"If Finn hears a word of this,"* ' he said to himself. 'Those were Coirpre's words. Well, he won't *hear* a word of it from me.' He took a knife from his belt and carved an ogham inscription on the log.

> While the salmon swims upstream,
> The cat grows fat on stolen cream

Not long after this, Finn was walking through the woods when he saw the log and read the inscription upon it. Finn knew what those words meant. Anger took him. He went home and confronted Lorna, who denied it all. Finn had no proof, and the matter was left unsettled. Things were cool between them after that.

Lorna was furious. She had lost the affection of her husband. He turned away from her in bed and would not take her out to feasts. It felt too risky to have Coirpre or any of her other friends over to visit. Her life was ruined; and she knew who was responsible.

Finn was out hunting one day. Coirpre came calling. Lorna told him he had to leave, and why, while the fool cowered in the corner.

Coirpre listened, twirling his moustache.

'Come with me, fool,' he said when Lorna had finished.

The trembling fool shook his head.

Coirpre seized his arm, pulled him up and dragged him out of the door. 'I was not here today,' said Coirpre to Lorna. She nodded.

He marched the fool out of the house. They walked through the woods until they were in a deep grove, far from any house. There, Coirpre told the fool to get to his knees.

The fool did so. He put out his tongue.

Coirpre laughed. 'I'm not going to cut your tongue out, you fool,' he said. Then he unsheathed his sword, drew it back and with a single swing, he severed the fool's head.

It hit the ground with a thud. Coirpre cleaned his blade on the grass and sheathed his sword. Picking up the fool's head by the hair, he set off home. He had some fun in mind.

When Finn came home after dark and asked where the fool was, Lorna said he had gone out walking.

'It's not like the fool to be out this late in the evening,' said Finn. 'I'll go and look for him.'

'No!' said Lorna.

Finn gave her a strange look. 'What do you mean, no?'

'I mean … I mean he went out to give us some time to our-selves. I asked him to go. I wanted to prove to you that you are the only man for me.'

'Oh,' said Finn with a smile. As wise as he was, love could always make a fool of him. 'And how might you do that?'

So things went as you might expect. Their door did not open that night or the next day. It was only as evening set in on that second day that Finn woke up with a start.

Lorna slept peacefully in his arms. Some dream had disturbed him, but it evaded his grasp. He only knew that it had been a dark dream, and that it concerned the fool.

Finn slipped from his wife's embrace. He knelt down in front of the fire pit and raked the ashes away, uncovering the glowing embers.

The Captain of the Fianna relaxed his eyes and gazed into the flames.

Their flickering became murmuring; their murmuring became whispering. Tears escaped Finn as the truth was revealed to him.

> Near to here, beneath the trees,
> Murder was done and now you see,
> Look how the fool's head rolled on the floor,
> The last time Coirpre passed through your door

Finn covered the embers. He dressed, armed himself and went outside. Putting the Horn of the Fianna to his lips, he blew it so hard that the stars shook.

Finn stood in the shadows, ravens gathering above him. He waited for the Fianna to rally and join him in his vengeance.

Meanwhile, at Coirpre's house, a feast was under way. The hall was bright with firelight. Meat smells and laughter filled the air. Coirpre had invited all his friends to join him, and they had come, for he held a good feast; the ale there never ran dry. They shared Coirpre's nature, and laughed as he boasted of taking Finn's wife in Finn's own bed, and in other places besides.

There was one, though, who did not laugh.

Closest to the door, furthest from Coirpre and in the place of least honour, was the fool's head. It had been mounted on a pike, and the pike driven into the earth so that it was level with the chests of Coirpre's friends. The fool's eyes were open, and they roved back and forth.

The feasters looked at the head and laughed as Coirpre told his tales, though some looked at it uneasily. After all, it was one thing to collect and display the head of a warrior vanquished in battle; it was another to display the head of a murdered fool. But they laughed along anyway.

Coirpre broke off his tale-telling to fill himself with meat and mead. His serving man went from place to place, heaping food on to every plate. Yet when he came to the fool, he served nothing. So Coirpre had ordered it, to dishonour the fool; but the fool would not tolerate it.

'What is this?' he said. 'Why has no meat been put before me?'

There were quiet noises of agreement. After all, the head had already been dishonoured; and this was far worse than being seated in the lowest place. This head had belonged to Finn's fool; at Finn's feasts, the fool would have sat at Finn's side. And now no meat was served to him! It was unwise to so dishonour the dead. Yet the mutterers did no more than mutter.

'You always have plenty to say, fool!' said Coirpre, juices dripping down his beard. 'If only you knew how to keep quiet. Perhaps I really should cut out your tongue!' Coirpre slapped his thigh and laughed. His friends laughed half-heartedly.

The fool grinned. 'Perhaps you should,' he said. 'Otherwise I might say this.'

> Wolves sing night-songs deep in the forest,
> Fat men feasting dishonour a fool.
> Coirpre's eyes will be eaten by rats,
> For he made an enemy of Finn MacCoull.

Coirpre's face soured. 'Hold your tongue, fool.'

'Why?' asked the fool. 'Or you'll cut it out and shove it somewhere dark? Finn will find it and beat you with it, and you will cry like a baby.'

At that Coirpre's friends couldn't help but laugh.

'Enough,' said Coirpre, pushing back his chair and drawing his sword. Down the hall he strode, shouting obscenities at the head; but the head only laughed, louder and louder.

Meanwhile, a sound reached the ears of the feasters. It was the distant sound of pounding feet, battle cries and swords beating against shields.

Coirpre grabbed the fool's head. He pulled it off its pike as the feasters stumbled to their feet and drew their swords.

'Into the fire with you, fool!' said Coirpre. But at that moment the door burst open and Finn and the Fianna charged in.

Coirpre dropped the head and drew his sword; but it did him no good. Finn and his men slew Coirpre and every man there.

After the fighting was over, Finn found the fool's head. He wept with it, laughed with it and took it to the Hill of Allen, where he gave it every honour.

❦

THE DAUGHTER OF KING UNDER WAVE

The wind howled like a god tormented. The waves rose up to strike the stars. Trees crashed to the forest floor and no beast nor man was abroad the night she came.

Three men of the Fianna had set out that morning; Finn, Ossian and Diarmuid. A storm was coming, but they had time yet, so they left their hunting cabin on the Isle of Skye and made for the Black Cuillin mountains. They jogged over the moors and foothills, Bran and Sceolan racing back and forth ahead of them. Bran startled a stag and the hunters gave chase, as the storm rolled over the ocean.

The wind blew harder and the rain fell thicker as the hunt went on. The hounds were quick, but not quick enough; the hunters were clever, but not clever enough. No matter which way they drove it, their prey evaded them, and as the autumn darkness gathered and the thunder groaned, they admitted defeat and trudged home.

There was no jesting, no singing in the cabin that night. In silence the hunters wrung out their wet clothes and prepared their meal while the hounds stretched out before the fire. They ate, drank and discussed the right and wrong moves of the day. The moaning of the wind turned to shrieking as they lay down beneath their sleeping skins around the fire.

Finn, Ossian and Diarmuid slept. Bran and Sceolan slept.

Wild was the storm's song, yet they slept deeply. So deeply that none of them awoke when in night's darkest hour, the door to the cabin swung open.

In walked the foulest woman in all the worlds. She was bent almost double; her hair was filthy and hung to the ground. Half her scalp was bald and flaps of skin hung from her face, revealing putrid flesh and yellow bone beneath. Her eyes were a milky white, and her jaw jutted forward like a serpent's snout.

She sniffed the air, ran her eye over the sleeping warriors and shuffled over to kneel beside Finn.

'Finn,' whispered the crone.

He opened his eyes, saw her and yelped with fright.

'Who are you?'

'An old woman in need of warmth, comfort and a man's strength. Let me in beside you.'

'No,' said Finn. 'I will not.' He closed his eyes and somehow managed to find sleep again.

The crone crept towards Ossian.

'Ossian,' she hissed.

Ossian opened his eyes.

'Poet,' said the old woman. 'Deer child. I am a woman in need of what a woman needs. Your father turned me away; he thinks me foul. Show that you are kinder. Let me in under your skins.'

But Ossian refused her.

So she shambled over to Diarmuid. Bran and Sceolan awoke, and whined as she passed.

'Diarmuid.' He opened his eyes. 'Let me under your skins.'

Diarmuid looked her over. Like the others, he was repulsed, but his kindness had its way. He allowed her in beside him. Once she was settled, he yawned and rolled away from her.

'Diarmuid,' she said.

'Yes?'

'I need more than to lie beside you.'

'What more do you need?'

'I want you to put your arms around me.'

Diarmuid didn't want to get closer. She was hideous and smelt

like an open grave. Yet his kindness had its way. He turned to face
her and put his arms around her.

He closed his eyes.

'Diarmuid.'

'Yes?'

'I need more than to have your arms around me. I need you to
kiss me.'

Diarmuid looked at her again. He did not want to kiss her.
Diarmuid was handsome – some said he was fairer than Finn – and
he was used to having his pick of the women at every feast. Yet, as
before, his kindness had its way.

He closed his eyes.

He leant forward, put his lips to hers and kissed her.

Retching and heaving, Diarmuid drew back and opened his eyes.

In his arms was the most beautiful woman he had ever seen.
He stared into her eyes and the world disappeared. There was no
storm, no cabin, no flickering fire; no Fianna, no Diarmuid, no
honour nor glory. There was only her.

She smiled at him. He smiled at her, and kissed her again, and
slept no more that night.

The next morning, Finn and Ossian awoke to find Diarmuid
gone. They were discussing the strange apparition they had both
seen in their dreams when the door opened, sunlight streamed in
and a beautiful woman entered the cabin.

Finn gawped. Ossian frantically thought of poetic words that
might win her heart. He was just opening his mouth to speak
when Diarmuid walked in, put his arms around the maiden and
kissed her.

Diarmuid turned to Finn and Ossian. 'My brothers,' he said.
'We have shared so many fine adventures together. I will always

remember you fondly, and all of the Fianna. But it is time for me to leave. This woman is to be my wife, and we are going away together.'

Finn and Ossian were so shocked that they could not bring themselves to argue. Besides, they were still dazzled by the beauty of the maiden; her hair that was stolen sunlight, and her eyes so deep that they could have drowned a god. So they accepted Diarmuid's good wishes, and wept as they watched him depart.

❧

The following days were a whirling dream of flower-strewn meadows, deep kisses, beds of moss and roofs of stars, as Diarmuid crossed the country with his bride. Diarmuid had known love, but never such a love, and the whole world seemed to be made just for them.

One day they came to a place by the sea. The sand was white, the water a perfect blue. Islands dotted the horizon while tree-clad mountains towered behind them.

'If I were to have a house anywhere,' said Diarmuid, 'I would have it here.'

'My love?' said his bride.

He looked at her. 'You do,' she said.

He looked back and saw a house, just where he had imagined it. Three hounds were running from the door towards them.

'This house is ours,' she said. 'It is my gift to both of us; on one condition. You must never, as long as we live, mention the way that I looked when I came to you.'

'Agreed,' said Diarmuid as the hounds reached them and leapt at him, their tails wagging. 'And you must never give away our hounds.'

'Agreed.'

And they went into the house together.

❧

❧

So a happy time came. Diarmuid and his bride ate together and walked in the forest together; they climbed the hills to watch the sunset and swam in the ocean at dawn.

It was the best time Diarmuid had ever known.

All too soon did it end.

Diarmuid was out fishing one day when someone knocked on his door. His wife answered the door, and there stood Finn.

'Finn MacCoull!' she said. 'It is an honour to have you here. Do come in and sit down; Diarmuid will be delighted to see you.'

So they sat and ate and drank and gossiped together, the hounds lazing before the fire, while they awaited Diarmuid's return.

Eventually Finn said, 'I'm sorry, but I cannot stay any longer. I'll come back to see Diarmuid another day. But before I go, can I ask you for something?'

'Anything,' she said. 'Anything Finn MacCoull asks for, I will give.'

'I would like one of those hounds.'

'Oh … but… well, you see…' she remembered what Diarmuid had said. Yet it was not done in those days to refuse anything a guest asked for. So she gave Finn one of their hounds, and Finn left with it.

Diarmuid came home. He kissed his wife, and asked where the other hound was, and she told him.

'You gave away my hound,' said Diarmuid, his face darkening. 'After you promised you would not! After I took you into my bed, and you a hideous, rotting hag –'

'That's once,' she said.

Diarmuid recovered himself, and vowed not to say such words again.

Time passed. One day, Diarmuid was out fishing again when there came a knock at the door. His wife answered, and there stood Ossian.

'Ossian!' she said. 'Finn's son, poet of the Fianna; what an honour! Please, come in …' so they sat together and passed the time until Ossian said, 'I am sorry, but I must go. First, though, may I ask you for something?'

'Of course.'

'I would like to have one of those hounds.'

'Oh … but …' and again, though she did not want to give away Diarmuid's hounds, she would not refuse a guest. So Diarmuid came home to find his hound gone, and he raged at his wife.

'How could you? I had only two hounds left, and now I have only one! After all I gave up for you, who was a hideous fiend when …'

'That's twice,' said Diarmuid's wife.

Days, weeks and moons passed. Diarmuid missed his hounds that were gone, but he loved the one he had left. It was rare for him to go anywhere without it, but on a day when he did, there came a knock at his door.

'Caoilte!' said Diarmuid's wife, when she saw who stood at her door. 'Come in, come in; you've just missed Diarmuid, but he won't be long …'

It wasn't long before Diarmuid came home. But when he did, Caoilte had already left; and the fleet-footed old warrior had taken Diarmuid's hound with him.

'My last hound,' said Diarmuid when he returned. 'I never should have taken you into my bed that night. You must have put a spell on me; otherwise I would never have shared my bed with such a filthy, ugly …'

The moment those words left Diarmuid's lips, a gust of wind blew. Diarmuid blinked, and when he opened his eyes, he was standing on long, green grass.

His house was gone. His wife was gone.

Diarmuid fell to his knees, howling his pain. When he opened his eyes, the first thing he saw was a drop of blood on a blade of grass.

He bent down, searched and soon found another drop, then another. Very soon, Diarmuid was on his wife's trail.

꩜

He followed it across Alba, back and forth, from west to east and from south to north, stopping only when it was too dark to see. Finally, the trail led him to a beach in the west, and he followed it until it reached the sea.

There, as Diarmuid looked out over the water, he heard a voice inside him, telling him what he must do.

Diarmuid walked into the water.

As he did, the water parted. A road appeared, leading under the waves, and he took it.

Diarmuid followed the road as it led him down, down, forever down, until he reached the Land Under Wave.

Above him, the sea. Beneath his feet, green grass. Diarmuid walked, and as he walked he began to see houses here and there, until he beheld in the distance a mighty city. At its centre was a castle of crystal and glass, and the castle pulled at his heart.

Diarmuid ran down the road, past folk fair and strange. He entered the city, reached the castle and was admitted to the chamber of the King.

The King Under Wave sat on his throne. Tentacles grew from his ears and elbows; crabs scuttled across his skin. Green and golden light shone through the walls, and by his throne, a fish-headed harper played.

'Sire,' said Diarmuid, bowing. 'I have a shameful tale to tell you.'

Diarmuid told his tale. When he had finished, the King spoke.

'Come this way,' he said.

The King Under Wave led Diarmuid up staircases and down corridors of gold, until they came to the highest chamber in the castle's spire. There, surrounded by white-clad nurses, lay his love, the Daughter of King Under Wave.

'She is dying,' said the King. 'And one only one thing can save her.'

'Tell me what it is, and I swear I shall fetch it,' said Diarmuid.

'It is the Cup of Healing,' said the King. 'It is far from here, across a swollen red river, and guarded by a Fomorian army. No one has gone from here to fetch it, for it is known that there is not a warrior beneath the sea who could do so.'

'I will fetch it,' said Diarmuid.

'You will not,' said the King. 'But it will do you no dishonour to try.'

Diarmuid made ready to go. Before he left the castle, the King said, 'I do not think you will return. But if you do, and the nectar from the cup restores her, know this: she shall hate you until the end of her days. Such is the price of its power.'

With those words like knives in his heart, Diarmuid departed.

He left the city; he left the Kingdom Under Wave. He ran and ran, for many days seeing no soul on the road. Singing whales soared above him, and the giants of the deep that prey on whales, and the beings of legend that prey on those.

Deeper and farther he went, and deeper and farther. When he lay down to sleep, he fell asleep to the King's words.

She shall hate you until the end of her days.

It couldn't be. He would save her, and she would surely love him again.

❧

At last, Diarmuid saw before him the river.

It was a river of boiling blood. It was so wide and so fierce that Diarmuid swore this was all the blood ever spilt in battle. There was no way he could swim across it.

Fresh bubbles broke the surface of the blood.

Something emerged. It was a man, a tiny red man, with twelve eyes that bore into Diarmuid.

'Diarmuid O'Duibhne!' said the man. 'The one the tales tell of.

❧

Friend of Finn, favourite of Angus; bearer of the Red and Yellow Spears. Diarmuid, who was cursed to be slain by the Black Boar. Do you wish to cross the river?'

'I do,' said Diarmuid.

The red man laughed, his twelve eyes rolling. 'So you seek the Cup of Healing. It is close, Son of Donn, Grandson of Duibhne; it is close. But you will not cross without my help.' As he spoke, he lifted from the bloody torrent an enormous red hand.

'Very well,' said Diarmuid. 'What price is your help?'

'Only this. That on your return – if you do return – you give half of the Cup's nectar to me.'

Because he had no other choice, and even though it might mean the death of his beloved, Diarmuid agreed.

He walked back, turned and ran at the river. He leapt and came down halfway across the river; but he landed on the red man's hand. The red man vaulted him up, far through the air and far past the river, and when Diarmuid landed, he found himself on a plain before a second mighty city.

Guards upon the towering walls saw him. They blew their horns, and other horns answered. There was the trooping of many feet, and the gates opened.

Out poured an army greater than Diarmuid had ever seen. Fomorian warriors in armour of every colour poured out of the city and took their place in ranks stretching on for miles. Warriors riding beasts of the deep, warriors carrying spears; warriors with swords and shields and huge twin-bladed axes. It took all day for them to assemble, and when they were done, there in the farthest depths of the ocean, they stamped their feet. They shook their spears. They waved their weapons and roared at Diarmuid, who stood alone.

He drew his sword. It had never sounded so lonely.

The horns sang, the army charged and Diarmuid emptied his mind of all but his love.

It was all he needed.

Like a scythe through grass; like a bull in its charge; like an arrow through the air, Diarmuid met the charge. Such fury had not been seen in the world since the gods themselves went to war. It was music, it was poetry, it was terrible and glorious; the death dance of Diarmuid O'Duibhne, that sent to the next world a legion of souls.

His work done, Diarmuid walked into the empty city. Through the streets he walked, until he came to a stairway leading down into the seabed. Down he walked, down and down until sweat dripped from his nose and the very rocks seemed to whisper.

At the bottom of the staircase, in a crystal chamber, he found the Cup of Healing. He picked it up and held it before his eyes, wondering at the power of the nectar it held, the light it cast upon the crystals of the cave.

Diarmuid turned and ran.

He bounded up the stairs and ran to the river. When he reached it he leapt to the other side; for Diarmuid was possessed of a new strength. Leaving the river and the angry cries of the red man behind him, he surged over the seabed until he reached the city, the castle, the chamber where his bride slept.

Terrified by the grey tint of her skin and the startling sound of her breath, he cradled her head in his hand.

He parted her lips.

Diarmuid put the cup to her lips … and stopped.

She shall hate you until the end of her days.

It wasn't true. It was a test of his love.

Diarmuid poured the liquid into her mouth.

She opened her eyes.

Colour flushed her cheeks as she gazed at him, her eyes full of love.

But only for a moment. A shadow passed over them, and they were full of hatred.

'Get out,' she said.

'But –'

'Get out. Never come here again, Diarmuid O'Duibhne.'

Diarmuid did not argue. He could not bear to hear any more. With one last look at her, he turned and walked away, down the stairs and out of the castle and the city. He was passing through the city gates when he heard behind him, 'Diarmuid!'

He turned. She was standing there, smiling at him.

Diarmuid went to stand before her.

'I do remember,' she said, her voice gentle. 'I remember all we shared. So let me give you this.'

She reached up and touched the tip of her finger to his brow. His forehead tingled, and he asked, 'What is that?'

'You will see,' she said. 'Go.'

So he left. As he walked, he looked back and saw her still standing there, smiling at him.

Diarmuid went back to the Fianna, and soon learnt what she had given him. It was a love spot. Any woman who looked upon it fell irrevocably in love with him. At first Diarmuid greatly enjoyed his love spot; but he soon took to wearing a cap to cover it up.

Diarmuid never saw the Daughter of King Under Wave again. He thought of her often, for as long as he lived. He would remember her standing at the city gates, smiling at him; and he always wondered whether she smiled because she had given him a blessing, or smiled because she had given him a curse.

THE CAVE OF KESHCORRAN

In County Sligo, the Hill of Kesh stands alone among rolling green fields. It is riddled with caves. Atop it one can see Queen Maeve's grave to the west, Sligo Town to the north-west and Ben Builben to the north. To the north-east is the plain of Moytura, where the battles between the Fomorians and the Tuatha de Danaan were fought.

In Finn's day, the slopes were covered in thick forest. It was a fine place for a hunt – as far as Finn knew.

Finn, Ossian, Goll and Conan took a group of Fianna there one misty spring morning. They blew their horns and bellowed so that the wild animals ran in fright through the forest. The Fianna split up and raced with their hounds beneath the branches. All was well; or so it seemed.

In truth, the Hill of Kesh was the worst possible place to hunt. It belonged to Conoran, a lord of the Tuatha De Danaan, who did not take well to men hunting on his hill without his permission. Conoran called his daughters to him and ordered them to punish the hunters. They were happy to oblige.

Conoran's daughters were not of ordinary appearance. Though they were beautiful of face and seductive of shape, their limbs were four times as long as their bodies, and their fingers and toes were four times as long as those of other women. They had a gift for weaving threads and a gift for weaving enchantments. These gifts, they now put to use.

The three sisters left the hall beneath the hill. They emerged at the mouth of a cave and set to work. Using yarns of silvery thread, they wove fine nets across the cave mouth.

That done, they sat back to wait.

Finn and Conan had been hunting together. Emerging from the forest, they found themselves at the mouth of the cave. They looked in wonder at the fine, shimmering threads. They forgot the threads as they stared at the women within the cave.

These were no ordinary women; that was clear. Yet there was something in their eyes, their smiles and their shape that pulled at Finn and Conan. They had long limbs, but what did that matter?

'Finn MacCoull,' said one of them, with wonder in her voice. 'And the mighty Conan MacMorna. It is an honour to see you at our door. It would be a greater honour to see you pass through it. Come, handsome warriors. Take a rest from the hunt. Enjoy some time with us.'

Finn and Conan thought that sounded like a fine idea. They could think of many ways to pass some time with these women. Dropping their catch, they clambered through the nets, and Conoran's daughters came forward on their long limbs and kissed them. Finn and Conan notice a strange tingling in their skin where they had touched the nets, but thought nothing of it.

The tingling spread. It became a numbness.

Finn and Conan fell to the ground. Their eyes were wide open; their limbs frozen.

The sisters laughed and dragged their catch into the depths of the cave.

Next came Ossian and Fergus of the True Lips. These two poets liked to hunt together, weaving words when they sat to rest.

They spied the cave. Within, the long-limbed women smiled at them. Poetry began to pour from the poets' mouths as they vied to best praise these strange beauties, who laughed and licked their lips.

'Join us, handsome poets,' they said. 'Let us taste your honeyed tongues.'

Ossian and Fergus climbed through the nets. Soon they were in the dark depths of the cave, prone and helpless.

❦

The day wore on. In twos and threes the hunters arrived at the cave; all of them accepted the sisters' invitation. Come dusk, almost the entire hunting party lay like corpses inside the cave, while outside their hounds howled.

The sisters looked at one another and laughed. Their work was done. It was time to feed.

They retreated into the cave. Arriving at the mound of hunters, they crawled across it, poking and prodding and licking their catch, laughing as they argued over which warriors would taste the finest.

Each sister selected a warrior to serve as an appetiser. It was time to begin the feast.

They sank their fangs into soft, warm stomachs. Flesh and muscle were torn between their teeth; still-beating hearts sent jets of blood streaming across the rocks. The sisters ripped and chewed and grew ever more frenzied; then froze.

A sound had reached their ears. A sound they did not expect to hear.

It was the unsheathing of a sword.

They leapt from atop the pile of warriors, bounded to the cave mouth and there, framed against the embers of the sun, stood Goll MacMorna, whom some called the Flame of Battle.

The sisters shrieked. Goll swung his sword, cutting through their webs. They emerged from the cave, hissing and snarling as they circled him.

Two of the sisters leapt at Goll. He swung his sword; their heads rolled across the grass.

❦

Goll faced the third sister.

She drew back. She was wary now. Slowly she and Goll circled one another, feinting and dodging. The sidhe had no sword, but her limbs were long, and she was quicker than any mortal. Goll knew he was in danger.

The sister darted forward. Goll swung his sword; but she was baiting him. She evaded his blade and sprang at him, knocking him to the ground.

Goll fought desperately to escape as her long limbs sought to bind him. Her reach was greater; but Goll wrestled every day. He slipped from her grasp, threw her down beneath him and tied her limbs with the straps of his shield.

The Flame of Battle raised his sword.

'Better you save your brothers,' said the sidhe, 'than deal death to me.'

'What do you mean?' asked Goll.

'The Fianna are within. Most are unharmed. Promise to spare me and I will restore them to life. Without the touch of my lips, none of your friends shall rise again.'

Goll wanted to make an end of her; but he knew he had no choice. He freed her feet, and at the point of his sword, she entered the cave, led him into its far reaches and climbed atop her catch.

'Wait,' said Goll, as she was about to kiss the first warrior. 'Free Fergus first. That one, there. Then Finn, then Ossian, then the others.'

She did as he asked before disappearing into the darkness.

Goll helped the Fianna to stand as they awakened. They were blood-soaked, cold and confused, and vowed never to hunt upon the Hill of Kesh again.

The hunting party returned to the Hill of Allen. Fergus of the True Lips wrote a poem praising Goll and his heroic deeds that day. The poem was popular and raised Goll's standing among the Fianna.

Just as Goll had intended.

THE HEALING
OF CAOILTE

Caoilte stumbled, fell and lay still.

From the wound in his chest ran a steady stream of blood. It soaked into the earth and Caoilte sighed as his pain eased. It would be easy to let his spirit drift off into the forest darkness, his body food for the crows.

Yes. He would do that. He would allow the threads of life to loosen –

A door opened in a nearby tree, splaying light over the old grey warrior's body.

'Caoilte?'

He did not reply.

Footsteps. Silence. More footsteps, voices. He was picked up and carried down stairs leading deep into the earth.

When Caoilte next opened his eyes, he lay in a bed in a candle-lit cave. Three people stood over him. One was Derg, his friend, whom he had been searching for. The other two were a man and woman with the look of the Tuatha De Danaan.

'You are lucky I came out and found you, old friend,' said Derg. 'You were on death's door as well as ours. You're close to it still.'

'Which is why I'm here,' said Caoilte. 'Word reached my ears that after leaving the Fianna, you joined the Children of Danu.'

Caoilte told Derg and his companions of how he had been wounded in battle by a spear thrown by Mane, Prince of the Fomorians. The poison was of a kind the Fianna had no cure for; so he had sought out Derg.

'And you assume we will help you?' said the woman. She was beautiful, thought Caoilte, as alluring as the forest night, yet there was something in her eyes that made him fearful.

'I am owed help,' said Caoilte, 'for I have given it.' He looked at Derg, and Derg nodded.

'That he has.'

'I was biding a time with Dubh and Don,' Derg said to his companions, 'of the Munster Tuatha De Danaan. Their clan was at war with a force of Fomorians. Every day we went out and fought them on the plain; every night we returned to our hall. We ate and drank, yet knew no rest; for every night our enemies sent to our hall a great bird. Bigger than a bull, with a beak of bone, it tore down the door and flew back and forth, shrieking and swooping down to tear open men, women and children.

'That bird would have been the end of us, if I hadn't sought out Caoilte. We were friends when I fought with the Fianna, and many times we darkened our spears together. I sought him out, found him and spoke of our plight. Caoilte came to our aid, carrying nothing less than the spear that brought down the fire-breathing sidhe at Tara.

'We waited in the hall. In the dead of night, when the bone-beak came, Caoilte rose with a roar, threw the spear and brought it down. If he had not, all our tribe would have perished. So I ask you, Bebind, to give him what he seeks.'

The woman, Bebind, gave Caoilte a long look.

'The poison is powerful, yet still he clings on,' she said. 'He is strong. Perhaps he could be of use.' She left, and returned bearing a golden cup full of ale. Intricate patterns lay upon the cup's surface, interlaid with gemstones of every colour.

'Do you know what this is?' Bebind asked Caoilte, who shook his head. 'It is the ale of Goibniu. The last medicine of the smith of the sidhe, and I am its keeper.' She leaned in close and smiled. 'I'll give it to you, old man,' she said. 'If you do something for us.'

'What?'

'Fight,' she said, her smile vanishing. 'For our clan is at war, and it is your fault.'

'My fault?'

'The fault of the Fianna. Ever since the Cup of Healing was taken by Diarmuid, the Fomorians have taken revenge on all Ireland. They have discovered where our hall lies, and tomorrow they will send an armada to land on our shores and breach our door. We will go out to meet them in battle, and you must join us. You must fight.

'Swear you will fight, and you will have enough ale to give you battle strength. Fight well, and I will give you more.'

Caoilte raged at Bebind. He called her all the foul names he knew. What kind of healer, he asked, withheld medicine from the sick? But

Bebind was unmoved, and his pain had returned. So he told her he would do whatever she asked, and she gave him a drink of the ale.

༄

The next morning, the sidhe left their hall. They reached the hilltop above the Bay of Kerry and looked out to sea.

The Fomorian fleet spanned the horizon. From their muster point on the Skellig Islands they came, riding the wind on sails woven from the skins of their enemies. Their battle chants froze the hearts of the Children of Danu.

'Their sorceress is with them,' said Cascorach the poet, who stood close to Caoilte. 'She is leading the singing.'

Cascorach raised his arms and began his own chant. The druids and poets of the time wove spells into their songs. In battles they clashed, putting courage into the hearts of their forces and fear into those of their enemies. They even struck at one another, for their most potent words charged the air like lightning, and their strike was just as deadly.

The waves of the sea swirled and hissed as Cascorach and the sorceress fought.

The Fomorians rowed for the shore.

The sidhe ran down the hill to meet them.

Caoilte laughed as he ran. The ale had worked well; his old strength filled his veins. Yet as he neared the bay and crossed the sand, he could already feel it fading.

By the time he drew his sword, he could taste blood in his mouth.

The armies met on the sand. Caoilte fought as he ever did, crying the war cries of the Fianna. That drew many enemies to him; the Fomorians hated any kinsman of Diarmuid. Caoilte dealt death to each one. He roared at the pangs of the poison and disguised his roars as battle rage.

༄

༄

All day the armies laboured upon the blood-soaked sands. Cascorach fought the sorceress from the hilltop; she flung spells from her ship.

The sun sank into the mouth of the west. Caoilte, heaving for breath and racked with pain, found himself surrounded by open space. The Fomorians around him had drawn back; they were laughing at him.

He turned around and saw why.

Ambling towards Caoilte was the King of the Fomorians.

Many of the Fomorians resembled men. Their King did not. He was monstrous, toad-mouthed and covered in green scales, with claws that could have cut iron. The King swished his tail, opened his mouth and roared a challenge that made Caoilte's ears ring.

Caoilte raised his sword.

The King raised his axe.

All fighting ceased as the armies gathered to watch.

The King ran at Caoilte and swung his axe. Caoilte leapt over the blow and over the King; the axe landed with a thud in the sand. The King roared, withdrew his axe, turned and swung again.

He was too slow. Caoilte was weakened; but he was still the fastest runner in Ireland. He had fought the King's son, the one who had given him his wound, and he knew how he must fight.

The King swung and swung, never catching Caoilte. As the King grew more frenzied, Caoilte began to dodge always in the same direction. The King grew dizzy, and at last fell to the ground.

Caoilte leapt upon the King, pulled back his head and cut his throat.

The Fomorians howled with pain and fear to see their leader vanquished. They fell into a rout, running for the shore and their boats. Up on the hill, Cascorach waited until they were all in the water, then turned the sea against them. The Fomorians drowned.

෴

෴

Caoilte was the hero of the hour. He was carried to the hall beneath the hill and blessed by every warrior before being led to his bed.

'You must be proud,' said Bebind, who was sitting on the edge of the bed, Goibniu the Smith's cup in her hands.

'Stuff pride. Give me the rest of that ale.'

'Caoilte,' she tutted. 'You should know better than to make demands of a woman of the sidhe.'

Caoilte thrashed as a fresh wave of pain assailed him. 'Please,' he said.

She put the cup to his lips. He drank all the nectar within it.

'It is not enough,' he said.

'I know,' said Bebind.

She lifted the covers from his bed. Delicately she lifted his shirt, exposing his spear wound, the skin green and black and purple around it.

Bebind had been smiling; the smile faded from Bebind's face. She leant down and put her mouth to the wound. Caoilte gasped as she sucked at it, drawing out the poison and swallowing it.

It was leaving him. Caoilte gasped; the poison was almost gone, he would be cured …

Bebind lifted her head and gave him a hard look. Poisoned blood dripped from her lips.

'No, swift one,' she said. 'Not yet. The Fomorians are not finished with us. They will attack again, and you will aid us.'

She turned and left. Caoilte screamed at her long after she was gone, and long after he knew he was screaming.

Time in a sidhe house cannot be measured, but it seemed a long time before Bebind came to Caoilte again.

'It has not been so long,' she said to him.

'Have you come to cure me?'

She did not answer. Instead she put a gaming board on his lap and began to arrange the pieces.

'What use have I for games, woman?' said Caoilte.

'You have a small mind, old man.'

'I'm younger than you, I'll wager.'

She smiled at that. 'Play with me.'

With nothing better to do, he moved his first piece.

'A wise move,' said Bebind, looking at him as if they shared a secret. 'A warrior has no weapon more powerful than his mind.'

She made her move; a good one. Caoilte's eyes roved the board, and he almost forgot his pain.

༄

Bebind often came to play with Caoilte after that. He enjoyed their games – he had nothing to do but wait for her to come – but he resented her for withholding his healing. The poison prowling through his veins grew stronger with each hour that passed.

A time came when Caoilte could no longer play games. All he could do was scream until he passed out, then waken to his own screaming. He saw Derg's face, and Bebind's and Cascorach's too, but whether they were real or phantoms he did not know; for he saw Finn, and Ossian, and Goll too, and others he did not know.

One day he saw Bebind's face. Again she was lifting his shirt, lowering her mouth to his putrid flesh, sucking forth the poison. It hurt, but he wanted the poison gone. And yet he wanted too to drift away, into the visions that came to him ever more often; of blue skies and whispering trees and hounds racing after white deer …

Bebind sat up. 'Not yet, old one,' she said. 'We still need one more favour from you.'

Caoilte was beyond protest. 'What do you need?' he asked.

'The Fomorians are threatening Ireland again. It is worse than it ever was before. They have summoned a vast flock of

༄

bone-beaked birds, just like the one that you slew. From west to east they turn the sky dark. The bone-beaks tear down halls and villages, and every evening they return to the west, carrying away children to be Fomorian slaves. Caoilte, you must defeat them.'

'I cannot even stand,' said Caoilte. 'What can I do?'

'I hope you find an answer to that,' said Bebind as she left.

The wind howled across the plain.

Caoilte had risen from his bed. Fallen. Risen again. Bebind had given him enough relief to enable him, in many fits and starts, to arm himself and leave the hall.

Sun-fire burnished the sky, bathing the fields and farmhouses in golden light. Caoilte stood alone, shivering, his cloak billowing, with one foot in life and one in death.

Were it not for what he saw in the sky, he would have gone joyfully into death. But he had work to do first.

Swarms of shrieking bone-beaks flew in circles above him. Every now and then, Caoilte saw one swoop down and rise up again, a child flailing between its talons.

It was time to end this.

But he did not yet know how.

A new kind of shrieking went up among the bone-beaks. He had been seen. They converged above him. At any moment they would dive and take him.

It was then that Caoilte noticed something dangling around his neck. A game-piece.

A warrior has no weapon more powerful than his mind.

Caoilte laughed. He took the piece from around his neck and knelt down in the long, damp grass. Among the grass was a gaming board.

So close to death, with the otherworld all around him, he knew what to do and had the power to do it. As the bone-beaks dived, Caoilte set his piece upon the board.

The bone-beaks became dust. Caoilte looked up and saw only the empty sky.

෯

Thus Caoilte ended the war with the Fomorians. He returned to Bebind's chambers of healing.

'Will you finish your work now?' he asked her.

'I cannot,' she said, stroking his grey hair. 'But another has come who will.'

Caoilte followed Bebind's gaze. His jaw fell open.

Into the chamber walked Cliodhna, Daughter of Manannan. Golden light lit the air around her, a gentle smile played about her lips, and around her flew the birds of the Land of Promise.

Caoilte closed his eyes as she and her birds began to sing. He flew far upon the wings of their song, to the Land of Promise and beyond. All the ages of the world passed as he wandered through palaces of dreams. When he returned, Cliodhna was gone, though Bebind remained.

She gave him new clothes, which were splendid even by the standards of the Tuatha De Danaan. After he had dressed, she led him out of the hall and into the forest, leading him to a waterfall pool hidden from mortal eyes.

A party of sidhe were swimming there, and Caoilte and Bebind disrobed and joined them. When they had finished swimming, they ate and drank upon the grass.

'You are free to go,' said Bebind to Caoilte. 'But I hope you will stay here with me.'

Caoilte was tempted by her offer, for now that the cloud of his sickness had cleared, he knew that he loved her. But his loyalty was to Finn, so he left Bebind and went to re-join the Fianna.

෯

THE RED WOMAN

One fog-mantled morning, in the feasting hall of the Hill of Allen, the men of the Fianna were doing nothing much at all.

A few sat at gaming boards. Conan was telling a war story but kept forgetting what happened next. His audience were only half-listening. Others simply stared into the flames of the fire. Bran and Sceolan looked up at Finn, their heads on their paws, seeming unimpressed by him and his company.

'Enough,' said Finn, clapping his hands together. 'Let's go hunting.'

A few men nodded, or made noises of agreement, but none of them stirred. Finn discerned that they needed the excitement of places unknown to them.

'We've seen enough of the forests around here,' he said. 'We'll hunt in Glen Smoll.'

The Fianna looked at one another. Glen Smoll? None of them had hunted there before. As one they rose and went to fetch their spears.

They crossed the country, made their camp and the next morning they set off hunting. Only a few steps had they taken from camp when they heard a heavy stamping sound.

The hunters paused. Watched. Waited.

Out of the undergrowth burst a creature of dreams.

It had the body of a deer and the feet of a man. Its head was that of a boar, with long, straight tusks, and on its flanks it bore crescent moons, which cast beams of dancing light through the dawn.

It was so wondrous that the hunters did not gave chase; they could only watch as it tore past them and disappeared into the foliage. They stared after the beast; then at each other; then at the one who came after it.

A woman emerged from the trees, seemingly on the trail of the beast. She had red hair, clothes, eyes and skin; she carried a red spear.

The red woman saw them and looked them over. She was about to carry on her way when Finn moved to stop her.

'Get out of my way,' she said.

'Which way is that?' asked Finn.

'I am hunting the beast,' she said. 'I see in your eyes that you have seen it. I must catch it, so step aside.'

'In that case, let us help you,' said Finn. 'I am Finn MacCoull, these are the Fianna, and if there is hunting to be done, we are the ones to do it.'

'Not today,' said the red woman. 'I have made a wager that I will follow this beast until it ceases to move, and if I fail in that, my life and the lives of my sons will be forfeit.'

'Then let us hunt alongside you,' said Finn.

'Step aside,' she said, and she thrust her spear forward. Its tip tickled Finn's throat.

Instantly the Fianna were around her, their spears aimed at her heart, their hounds baring their teeth. Finn opened his mouth to speak, thinking to calm the red woman and his warriors, but the red woman spoke first.

Serpentine words danced from her tongue, making the air pulse and shimmer. A moment later she was no longer a woman but a giant red snake, her coiled body as thick as an oak.

The red snake raised her head, hissing at Finn who stared up at her, transfixed. Her head danced back and forth and so did Finn's. At any moment she might strike and take Finn's head between her teeth.

Bran and Sceolan attacked at once. Bran leapt for her throat; Sceolan lunged and bit into her tail. The serpent writhed and threw Sceolan off. She wrapped Bran in her coils, squeezing her tightly enough to crush her bones.

CRGD

Finn's sword point appeared at her throat.

'Release her,' said Finn.

'Release me,' hissed the snake.

Finn lowered his sword. The serpent became a red woman again. Bran raced for cover.

'Very well. If you can keep up, you can hunt,' said the red woman before disappearing into the green.

The Fianna looked at one another, grinned and ran after her.

All day they tailed the beast, the red woman always in front of them. Though they were hungry, they did not stop to eat; when they were thirsty, they did not stop to drink. They stayed instead on the trail of the beast, wild with lust for its capture.

The sun fell. The night was dark, and any other hunt would have ended. But the moons on the beast's flanks cast an ethereal light that reached up to the stars and across the earth, bathing the forest in silver. The night was a dream, a story each hunter would tell until his dying day, and not one man complained, or let himself fall behind. Their heartbeats became pounding drums, their laboured breath a rapturous song as they ran on and on through the night forest.

The moon reached its zenith. Up ahead, the beast gave a cry that warned them away and urged them on.

The ground grew wet beneath their feet. In the unearthly light, the hunters saw that their boots were bathed in blood.

The hounds grew frenzied. They reached open ground and saw the beast atop a mound, the red woman not far behind it. Torrents of blood shot from each of its moons, drenching the forest from the grass to the treetops, yet it stood tall and seemed unharmed. The Fianna laughed and resumed the chase.

Come dawn, the beast was gone. A bright sun rose, the hunters slowed and they saw before them a hillside. A door led into the hill, and the red woman stood before it. She was soaked in blood, panting for breath and smiling at them.

'Not bad,' she said. She glanced towards the door. Finn heard from within the distant sound of music and laughter. 'The hunt is over. I followed the beast all the way to this door, where we bowed to one another; thus I saved my sons. Now I go inside to celebrate. Will you join me?' she asked, her eyes upon Finn.

'We cannot go to a feast looking like this,' said Finn, indicating his men and their blood-drenched clothes.

The red woman took a horn from her belt and blew on it. The door opened, and out came ten young men of the Tuatha De Danaan.

'Sons of Danu,' she said. 'Bring the Fianna hot water to wash in, and new clothes to wear.'

The young men left and soon returned with basins of steaming water. The Fianna removed their clothes and bathed before dressing in the clothes the young men handed to them.

'Follow me,' said the red woman, and they followed her into the hill.

Within the hill was a hall of the Children of Danu. It blazed with light and was filled with beautifully attired women and men, all of whom were eating and drinking or dancing and singing. The red woman led Finn and the Fianna through the throng to where the King sat. They bowed to him, and a table was laid out for them at his side.

The feast went on in the way of feasts beneath the world, where the passing of days is a faraway thought. Eventually, the red woman rose and addressed the King.

'I think Finn MacCoull and his men would like to see the beast,' she said.

The King clapped his hands. Straight away the congregation fell silent.

The red woman took a wand from within her gown and struck the wall. A door of thick oak and golden latticework appeared there, and all watched as it opened.

Through it came walking the beast.

Not a whisper broke the silence as the beast strode through the hall, turning this way and that, allowing the assembly to marvel at it. The light from its twin moons lit up the hall and was reflected in every jewel and every pair of eyes.

The beast spoke.

'I enjoyed my time and the hunting here,' it said. 'Now I must leave and make for my own country.' It looked at Finn. 'I am the fastest runner beneath the sky. Land and sea are the same to me. I challenge you to chase me as I make my way west, and bring me down before I leave you forever.'

To that, Finn and all the folk there agreed.

❦

The hunt began on the hillside above. Renewed by rest and feasting, the Fianna and their hounds tore ahead of the Children of Danu, pursuing the beast far across the country. Whenever they reached a hilltop, they would look to the western sea, and see that it had drawn closer. When the beast reached the sea, it would be lost to them for good.

Onwards they went, though they were tiring now. All of them but Bran. Finn's favourite hound was always ahead, always urging on the others, and as the sun began to sink, she glimpsed the beast up ahead.

Bran reached a patch of thick forest. She knew the beast would be forced to slow as it found its way forward. Not Bran; she was smaller, and not even the beast was better than her at slipping

❦

through the densest growth. She smelt that the beast was close, and howled for Sceolan to join her.

She had the beast within sight. She had the beast within reach.

Sceolan was with her, circling ahead. Bran lunged at the beast, forcing it towards Sceolan. Sceolan threw himself at it, it dodged away but Bran was waiting. She flew at the beast and closed her jaws upon its throat.

The Fianna arrived soon afterwards. They were so close to the sea that they could hear the beat of the surf. Bran and Sceolan lay panting, their prey between them. Yet it was not the beast that lay dead upon the grass. It was a man, his skin a deep blue with strange symbols marking it.

The red woman arrived.

'Is this the beast?' asked Finn.

'It is and it is not,' said the red woman. 'For the beast was in truth the King of the Firbolgs, one of the races that lived in Ireland before the coming of the Children of Danu.'

She turned to look at Finn, taking his hand in hers as the rest of the Fianna and the other hunters from the hall arrived.

'The Firbolgs will not forget this. Ireland will burn as they take their death price. Come away with me.' She stroked his hand. 'I go now across the waves, to Tir Nan Nog. Live with me in peace and plenty, in splendour and celebration, and never grow old.'

Finn looked at his men, who were watching him intently. Perhaps they were remembering when he forgot them in his passion for Sabha, or how Lorna had deceived him. He knew that for all his wisdom, a fair face was all it took to make a fool of him.

Finn smiled at her. 'It is a fine offer,' he said. 'But I would not give up Ireland, or the company of the Fianna, if I were to get all the lands of men in exchange, and the Country of the Young with them.'

So the red woman said goodbye to Finn, and went over the sea to Tir Nan Nog. Finn and his men returned to the Hill of Allen, grateful for the adventure and the story they would tell of it.

৩৯৩

FINN & THE PHANTOMS

In days gone by, Ireland was divided into four provinces: Connacht, Ulster, Leinster and Munster. The men of Munster were known for having fine horses.

Finn heard there was to be a fair in Clochair in Munster, and decided to attend. He invited his son Ossian, and Ossian invited his own son, Oscar, who was growing tall and strong and was known for his kind and happy heart.

They travelled across the country, arrived at the fair and were warmly welcomed by the Munster men. By night they ate and drank, told stories and heard new ones. By day they raced horses, thundering over the fields. There was a man present at the fair called Fiachu. He was the son of Eoghan, who had been a man of the Fianna for a time and a close comrade of Finn. Fiachu was wealthy, and on the last day of the fair, he presented Finn, Ossian and Oscar with three beautiful black horses. The warriors of the Fianna were overjoyed, and after thanking Fiachu and saying their goodbyes, they rode their new horses away from the fair.

They rode until they came to the Strand of Berramain, a stretch of sand that goes on for miles. The warriors raced there, whooping and laughing as their steeds showed their worth. They raced faster than thought over the golden sands, bathed in the fires of the setting sun.

At the end of the beach they did not stop. Day turned to night as they raced up the Hill of Bairneth, only stopping when they spied a house among a grove of holly trees.

๛

It was no ordinary house.

Its appearance was that of an ordinary house. But from within it came a cacophony of screams, groans and wretched sounds that made the horses whinny and the warriors wonder if this was a good place to stop.

'Are we stopping here for the night?' asked Oscar.

'It does not seem a welcoming place,' said Ossian. 'Yet I am intrigued as to what might await us inside.'

'Let us go in,' said Finn. 'This is a strange place, and it is good to have knowledge of strange things.'

The three warriors dismounted. They approached the door, and Finn gave three knocks.

The screaming ceased.

The door swung open.

Stood there was a small, hunched, grey-skinned man, his eyes wild and his beard dangling between his knees.

'What's this?' he said. 'Finn MacCoull, if I'm not mistaken; and his son Ossian, and Ossian's son Oscar. What an honour! Come away in and make yourselves at home; bring your horses in, there's room for them too.'

They did as bidden. Once inside the house, they looked around.

It was dark. The fire at the centre of the room had faded to embers. By the dim ember light they saw, sitting on furs at the fireside, an ancient three-headed hag, her three toothless mouths smiling at them. Old as she was, she wore a sword at her waist.

Beside the hag sat a man who had no head at all, though he did have a single, huge eye in the centre of his bare chest that roved back and forth over them. He wore an axe at his waist.

'An honour it is, a great honour,' said the old man. 'Now, to demonstrate the hospitality of this house. Hospitality worthy of such guests; hospitality such as they have not seen before.

'First, we must make our guests comfortable. Sit here, mighty warriors.' He gestured, not to the rugs and furs around the fire, but to some hard wooden boards in the corner of the room. It wasn't what their visitors had hoped for after a day in the saddle, but they would not refuse hospitality, so they sat down, their rears complaining.

'Warmth!' said the old man. 'We must make our guests warm, and ward off the night's chill.' He went to a wood basket, took some logs and set them on the fire. Finn sighed with relief; it would be good to feel warm. Yet the wood was elder wood, and soon the house was filled with thick, dark smoke and the warriors were coughing and spluttering.

'Well,' said the old man, his grey eyes shining. 'Comfort and warmth are all very well, but we must cater for the mind as well as the body. Let us have music.'

He clapped his hands. From the dark recesses of the smoke-addled room rose a host of corpses, rotting flesh hanging from their bones.

'Sing, my friends!' cried the old man. 'Sing!'

So the corpses sang, and it was the worst singing the warriors had ever heard. The hag joined in too, each of the heads singing a different hideous song to a different hideous tune, while the headless man clapped his hands, out of time, his great bulging eye fixed on his visitors.

'Enough,' said the old man. 'Fine music indeed, I'm sure our guests will agree. But now it is time to eat.'

The corpses fell silent and sank to the floor. Finn, Ossian and Oscar sighed in relief; then watched in horror as the headless man with the eye in his chest rose up and took the axe from his belt. He went to where the horses stood and swung his axe.

The horses brayed in terror. They lashed out with their hooves but it did no good. He moved like smoke among them, cutting through their legs and hacking at their haunches until the black Munster horses were bloody piles of flesh.

Finn and his companions looked on and did nothing. As much as the sight pained them, no man of the Fianna would ever refuse food from his host.

When the bloodshed ceased, the house's occupants took sharpened sticks from the fireside. They used them to spear chunks of horseflesh, held the chunks over the fire, and after only a few moments, offered the meat to their guests.

'Enjoy your meal, friends,' said the old man.

The warriors could not refuse. Finn took a skewer of meat and put it to his mouth.

It was raw.

When Finn MacCoull tasted the raw flesh of his own horse in his mouth, his patience came to its end.

'I will not eat this,' he said.

'You will,' said the grey man. 'You will not let it be said that the Fianna refused hospitality.'

'Hospitality?' said Oscar. 'What have we done to deserve such hospitality as this?'

Those were the words their hosts had been waiting for.

The meat was thrown aside. The grey man, the hag and the headless man drew their weapons.

Finn, Ossian and Oscar leapt up and unsheathed their swords.

'You don't recognise us, do you, Finn?' said the grey man, his dagger shining amid the smoke.

'I think I would remember you,' said Finn.

'Maybe,' said the old man. 'Yet we are not as we once were. We were once fine-looking young folk. Grief aged us, Finn. Anger broke us, and black spells remade us.

'We are the brothers and sister of Cuillen, Princess of Munster. Cuillen was the mother of Fear Og. Surely you remember him.'

'He served with us awhile,' said Finn. 'He was a good man, and I liked him well.'

'But your brothers didn't, did they, Finn?' said the old man. 'For he always was first in the hunt. The winner of every game; the man who could answer any riddle. He had your friendship and love, and for all that, the Fianna envied him.'

'So he left the Fianna,' said Finn. 'I remember. It does not make me proud.'

'You think the story ends there, Finn MacCoull,' said one of the hag's heads. 'It does not; for their envy had power. It poisoned him. After he left the Fianna, Fear Og took ill and died.'

'I am sorry,' said Finn.

'We buried him,' said another head, 'and his mother keened over his grave. Her grief song did not end that day or that night. She keened him for a year, until at last she fell dead upon her own son's grave.'

Finn opened his mouth to speak, but could not.

'We buried her there, next to her son,' said the last head. 'And the road we took from that day led us here.'

'And it led Finn and his kinsmen here too,' said the old man. 'To meet their end.'

He spoke words of magic, surrounding the warriors with bitter smoke. Through the smoke he and his brethren came, howling battle cries. They surrounded the warriors, swinging their weapons with skill. Finn, Ossian and Oscar were pressed back.

The night wore on. The fighting did not slow. Finn and his men were tired but forced themselves to fight on. The hosts drew back, but the corpses replaced them, attacking with fists and crude weapons. Ossian was wounded, then Oscar, and the hag's heads laughed as victory drew close.

Yet Finn did not falter. Though he was oldest, he knew fighting in a way they did not; he knew where his deepest wells of strength lay. Finn fought on as Ossian and Oscar fell back. He cut through the corpses and assailed the hosts. Finn thrust his sword forward, aiming at the headless man's giant eye, just as the sun crept over the horizon outside.

In an instant, the house vanished. The hosts vanished, and the corpses too, leaving Finn, Ossian and Oscar alone upon the cold, windy hill.

They limped away in search of warmth and food.

That evening, they were quiet at the camp. They were weakened, sore and sorrowful for the sad fate of Fear Og and his mother Cuillen. They grieved, too, for Cuillen's brothers and sisters, and the path their grief and hatred had led them down.

THE HUNT OF
SLIEVE CUILLIN

As soft as fawn skin was Finn's whistle, calling Bran and Sceolan to him.

He listened for them while keeping his eyes on the grey fawn at the end of the meadow. Ears pricked, eyes wide, it searched for the source of the danger it sensed.

Bran and Sceolan burst from the bushes. The fawn bounded away and Finn raced after his hounds.

North from the Hill of Allen it led them. Dawn became day; day became dusk. Out of Leinster they passed, into Ulster and to the hill of Slieve Cuillin that stands by the shore.

In the woods near the peak, Finn and his hounds lost their quarry. They stood, panting, looking at one another. Were they going to give up? No. The fawn was going to fill their bellies that night. Bran and Sceolan set off west in search of it; Finn set off east.

He walked beneath oak and ash and rowan until he came to a lake. Sitting beside it was a young woman with dripping wet hair, wearing a gown of green and gold.

Finn walked over to her and said, 'Good day to you.'

The young woman stared into the still water.

'I don't wish to trouble you,' said Finn. 'But I wonder if you saw a grey fawn pass this way. I was on its trail and lost it.'

'Keep your cares to yourself,' said the woman. 'I have my own.'

She turned and fixed Finn with a fierce stare. 'If there was one thing in the world that I valued, it was my ring of red gold. I lost it when I was swimming in the lake, and now I place you under a geis to find it for me.'

Finn smiled and cursed inwardly. In those days, when a lady put a geis, or bonds, upon a warrior, it meant that he must do whatever she ordered, or forfeit his honour – and perhaps even his life. Finn would never refuse a geis, so he stripped to the waist and waded into the lake.

Under the surface he went. He swam about the lake, blind in the murky waters, until at last he clasped the ring between his fingers.

Finn surfaced, called to the woman and swam towards her. She leapt up and ran to the water's edge.

Dripping and panting, the ring in his hand, Finn waded towards the edge. The woman waded towards him.

'There's no need for you to get wet,' said Finn. 'You can stay there and keep your clothes dry.'

She didn't seem to hear him. Her eyes were hungry as she splashed through the water.

Finn held out his hand, offering her the ring of red gold.

She took it, dived into the water and was gone.

Gone.

Not a ripple broke the surface.

Finn was alone.

He waded out of the lake, though it seemed a great effort to do so. He was tired, he supposed, from the long hunt and his swim. But why was he was so, so tired?

With all his will he forced himself to take the long walk out of the water, to a stone at its edge. He sat down, grateful yet wincing as his bones were complaining now. Shivering uncontrollably, Finn looked down at his hands.

They were the hands of an old man.

He brought his hands to his face.

It was the wrinkled, thin-skinned face of an old man.

Finn untied his fair hair.

It was the white, thin hair of an old man.

The woman must have been one of the sidhe; she had laid some spell upon him. What to do? He decided to wait for Bran and Sceolan to find him. They would lead him to help, or lead help to him.

Yet when Bran and Sceolan came bounding out of the bushes, they did not know Finn, and went onwards without him.   Finn sat there alone, fearful of the cold, oncoming night.

༨༨༠

Back in Finn's fort a few days later, a group of men had gathered for a feast. The meat was piled high, yet they were in low spirits, wondering what had happened to their leader. Conan MacMorna was not worried, though; he was deep in his cups and full of mockery.

'Look at you all,' laughed Conan, pouring another ale. 'Finn goes away for a few days and you are all fretting like nursemaids! If he cannot survive for a few days without us, why should we follow him?'

'He only went out hunting,' said Caoilte. 'He should be back by now. I have a feeling some dark work has been done.'

'If he is so mighty, he will make it home,' said Conan. 'If not, then we are well rid of him and can choose a new leader.'

The other men decided to go out and find Finn. They left and Conan came with them, bringing a skin full of ale. Their hounds found Finn's trail and it led them north, all the way to the lake atop Slieve Cuillin.

An old man sat on a stone there. He stared into the water and would not meet their eyes.

'Old man,' said Caoilte. 'Did you see a fair-faced man and a handsome pair of hounds pass this way?'

'I did,' wheezed the old man. 'They have not long left me.'

'Well,' said Caoilte. 'Where did they go?'

'Where indeed,' said the old man with a sad smile. 'Where indeed.'

༨༨༠

Caoilte bristled at that. 'Look here,' he said. 'That fair-faced man is dear to me. I would know what became of him, and you would be wise to tell me.'

So Finn told him, and Caoilte could not speak for grief.

'It is a great shame, what has happened to you, Finn,' said Conan. 'And you were once so pretty! As fair as you are now haggard. Perhaps it is justice.'

'What madness has taken you?' asked Caoilte.

'If you were a Son of Morna, you would not ask that,' said Conan with a belch. 'Finn was always our enemy. He claimed to leave the past behind when he took the captaincy from my brother. But he has ever slighted us, seated us in low places and offered us the worst spoils of battle.' Conan put his hand on his sword hilt. 'I say it is time we put the old fellow out of his misery.'

'I will put you out of your misery,' said Caoilte, drawing his own sword.

'Enough!' said Finn, his voice rasping. 'This is sorcery, done by a daughter of Cuillin, the sidhe of this hill. If you wish to help me, you must find a way into the hill and force Cuillin to undo his daughter's work.'

Conan opened his mouth to argue.

Caoilte drew his sword, and so did all the others.

'No sun rises that does not set,' said Conan. He wandered off into the forest to finish his ale.

The rest of the warriors searched for an entrance to the sidhe hall. Finding none, they began to dig into the hillside with rocks and their bare hands. They worked for days, until at twilight on the fourth day, a door appeared in the hill close to where they worked. It opened and out walked Cuillin himself, the lord of the hall. He wore a green cloak lined with red fur, and his eyes sparkled like emeralds.

'Guardians of Ireland,' he said. 'My daughter has admitted what she did to your leader. I have no quarrel with you, Finn. Take this.'

He offered a vial of liquid to Finn.

Finn drank it down greedily. The moment he did, the years fell from him and he was himself again; as fair as the sunrise after a storm.

But for his hair.

No matter what words he or his druids spoke; no matter how hard he wished; Finn's hair remained silver after that day. Some told him he looked better that way, wise and distinguished, but he never believed them.

PART III

DIARMUID & GRAINNE

THE WEDDING

Across Ireland and Alba, in the halls of lords and the huts of herds-men, tales were being told of Finn MacCoull. His fame surpassed that of his father and every captain of the Fianna before Coull. Winters came and went as bards recited the stories of Finn and Sabha, Finn and Finegas, Finn's fool and Finn's meeting with the red woman. Children played at being Finn, while men and women, facing hardships, asked themselves what Finn would do.

And as for Finn himself?

Finn was growing old. He never slept through the night; his bones ached through the frosty winters. His sword weighed heavily in his hand, and he practised with it less and less, preferring instead to watch the younger men spar, wrapped in a warm cloak beside the other greybeards.

All this would have been well. His men loved him fiercely and he had nothing to prove to himself or history. Only one thing was wrong.

Finn had no wife to share his bed.

He had bound himself to a bride more than once in his life. There had been beautiful Sabha, cruel Lorna, wise Oona and others besides them. But even the best of memories fade, and now Finn found himself wishing for a companion to share his twilight years with.

Yet who would take a man his age? No, better not to seek a wife, he told himself. He had his son Ossian, his grandson Oscar, his friends Diarmuid and Caoilte and many others. It was more, much more than enough.

Yet still he yearned, and one day, out on the green meadows of Allen, Finn said to Ossian and Oscar, 'I would like to take a wife.'

They were pleased, for they had sensed this need in him. When he voiced his fear that he was too old, they would not hear it.

'You are Finn, son of Coull,' said Ossian. 'There is no better man in Ireland or Alba than you, and no woman who would not want you. The question here is which woman is worthy of you.' Ossian had been thinking on this subject, and was not slow in answering his own question. 'There is only one woman worthy of marrying my father.'

'Who is that?' asked Finn.

Ossian smiled. 'Grainne,' he said. 'Daughter of the High King of Ireland.'

Finn had heard of Grainne. Everybody had. Her beauty was fast becoming legendary, and she was known to sing as sweetly as the summer rain.

'They say her smile lights up a hall like a star fallen from the sky,' said Oscar.

'I've heard her spirit is that of the wildcat,' said Ossian, 'that roams fierce and wild through Alba's glens.'

Finn was intrigued. He felt his heart quicken. She sounded like exactly the kind of woman he liked. Yet Grainne was young, and he was old; could it work between them?

'Let us ask her for you,' said Ossian. 'If she says no, she says no, and if she says yes, you will make her glad of it.'

Finn took a deep breath. He looked up at the sky, down at the earth and at the loose strands of his silver hair, dancing in the breeze.

'Ask her,' he said.

❧

So Ossian and Oscar travelled to Tara. They stood before the High King in his hall and asked for Grainne's hand for Finn.

❧

The King was surprised, for Finn had been a warrior when he himself was still a boy. Yet he liked Finn, and knew that he would be kind to Grainne. So he thanked and dismissed his visitors, and called in Grainne to tell her of Finn's proposal.

'I have heard many tales of Finn,' said Grainne, 'but I have never met him. They say his best days are behind him.'

'The worst days of Finn will be better than the best days of other men,' said the King. 'I think it is a good match.'

Grainne knew her father cared for her. She also knew his name would be better remembered, should she marry the Captain of the Fianna. As for herself, she was wary yet intrigued. To marry Finn MacCoull! She would be the envy of every woman beneath the sun. He might not be as young as some men, but if he was proposing to marry a maiden such as she, he couldn't be all that withered. She could sit by his side, among the first of the Fianna, and her name would be known for as long as his own – until the end of days.

'Very well,' she said to her father. 'I will marry Finn MacCoull.'

The news was delivered to Ossian and Oscar, who sent messengers to the Hill of Allen with instructions to prepare for a wedding. It was decided that the two warriors would escort Grainne to Allen, and that the wedding would commence when she arrived.

The travellers took the road south to Allen. As they walked, and by the fireside in the evening, Grainne heard her favourite tales from the men who had lived them. She laughed, wept and grew eager to arrive at Allen and be wed to Finn.

The journey from Tara to Allen is not a long one. Very soon they saw the hill, and the white fort atop it, and heard the horns that announced their arrival.

In his chambers, Finn was given the news; his bride would be there soon. Yet again, he looked in the looking glass. His skin was no longer smooth. His hair was no longer fair. Could a maiden love a man like him?

No, a voice whispered in his mind. She could not. He would repulse her. She would love his name, not him.

I am my name, Finn told himself. The stories spoken of him were true. He had always been open-handed; never had he run from battle. He would have to impress that upon her, dazzling her with his fame, so she would be sure to overlook his age. He was a good man, he would be kind to her and she would be happy.

Dressed in a wolf-fur cloak, Finn left his chambers.

He went to the feasting hall and sat in the high seat. Servants bustled back and forth as hundreds of warriors took their places, meat smells thick in the air. When all were seated, at a nod from Finn, the chief bard began to pluck his harp. He played a piece worthy of the harpers of the sidhe, and at its crescendo, the doors opened.

In walked a woman who turned all else to grey shadows. She wore a green gown, a jewelled belt and a circlet of gold. Her features were those of the Children of Danu, yet even more sensuous; even more suggestive of gentleness and strength, of wildness and wisdom, of poetry and passion and worlds beyond the world.

Finn realised she was standing in the middle of the hall, looking expectantly at him. She was waiting for him to welcome her, as was everyone else.

He rose from his seat, fearing he had looked foolish. Everyone was smiling. Were they laughing at him? Did they think that he was too old for her, that his heart would stop when she kissed him? Did she think that? Should he cross the room to speak to her, or summon her to him?

Finn pushed his doubts aside. It was important that he look impressive to her.

'Come here,' he said.

Her smile disappeared for an instant. It reappeared and she crossed the hall to stand before him. Finn descended the steps and faced her.

'My son is the greatest poet in Ireland,' he said. 'Yet his words could not do your beauty justice.' Grainne's smile widened. He was doing better.

'Before we are wed,' Finn continued, 'I must ask you certain questions.

Grainne's smile fell. 'Then ask them,' she said.

'What,' said Finn, 'is whiter then snow?'

'The truth,' answered Grainne.

'What is the best of jewels?'

'A knife.'

'What is hotter than fire?'

'The face of an honest man, when a stranger arrives at his door and he has no food or drink to give him.'

'And what,' asked Finn, 'is quicker than the wind?'

'A woman's mind,' said Grainne.

Finn smiled. 'Fine answers,' he said. 'And you will make a finer wife. Let us feast tonight, and join our hands in the morning.'

So Grainne took her seat beside Finn, and the feast began.

As the Fianna ate and drank, they took turns to stand before Finn and Grainne and pay their respects. Finn introduced her to Goll, Black Gary, Caoilte and many others. She smiled and thanked them for their good wishes while inwardly she seethed.

Finn was not the man the bards sang of. His hair was grey, not fair. He was not humble or kind; he was aloof and arrogant. Why must she answer his questions? Was she not the Daughter of Ireland's King, and he an old man? Better she had won Ossian, or Oscar, or a hundred other men. Anyone but Finn.

As the night wore on, she found her eye always returning to one man. He had black hair, ruddy cheeks and a smile that made her smile whenever she saw it. He wore a cap pulled down low over his forehead. It was clear that the Fianna loved and esteemed him, yet he never went far from the door.

'Who is that man?' she asked Ossian. 'He has not come to greet me.'

'That is Diarmuid O'Duibhne,' said Ossian. 'Finn's greatest friend. My father has charged him to watch over the feast tonight, and over you.'

Better I had married Diarmuid, she thought.

The night wore on. The air grew thicker with smoke and smells, song and laughter. The men argued and wrestled and stole lusty glances at Grainne.

A burst of barking and growling cut the songs and laughter short. A slab of meat had been tossed to the hounds, which set to fighting for it. Most of the warriors stepped back to let nature take its course, while others ran in to break up the fighting.

One of these was Diarmuid.

Grainne watched as Diarmuid waded in, pulling the hounds apart. She watched as his cap fell from his head.

He looked up.

Looked at Grainne.

Their eyes met. She looked above his eyes, at the dark spot on his forehead, the gift that the Daughter of King Under Wave had given him.

The love spot.

Grainne, the moment she looked upon that spot, fell in love with Diarmuid; and no mind ever worked quicker than hers did as she plotted how to make him her own.

❦

'My darling,' Grainne said to Finn, who was looking sleepy. 'I have with me a jug of mead. I wish to offer a toast to our marriage, to be drunk by all who are present.'

❦

Grainne didn't mention that her old nurse had given her the mead, to offer to Finn on the nights when his affection was unwanted.

'Very well,' said Finn.

So Grainne fetched the jug of mead. She waited until Diarmuid, his cap back upon his brow, was out of the hall. The moment he left, she went around pouring a little mead into every cup. She toasted Finn, she toasted their marriage, the Fianna cheered and drank ... and fell asleep, their heads crashing upon the tabletops.

Diarmuid returned from the wash house and entered the silent hall.

He saw the guests sleeping with their heads in their food. The hounds ran back and forth about their feet. The fires burned, Finn slept in his chair and Grainne stood alone in the middle of the hall, her eyes looking into his.

'What sorcery is this?' asked Diarmuid.

'The oldest spell of all,' said Grainne. 'Love.'

Diarmuid's heart sank as his fears were confirmed. Finn's bride had seen his love spot.

'Listen to me,' he said. 'I know you believe you love me –'

'I do love you,' said Grainne. 'And I declare that I will not marry Finn, tomorrow or any other day.'

'Finn is my captain and friend –'

Grainne stepped forward, no longer smiling.

'Finn is old, and proud, and unworthy of me,' she said. 'Leave with me, and I will give you my love, tonight and all of our days.'

'Grainne –'

'Come away with me,' she said. 'I do not ask. I put you under bonds, Diarmuid O'Duibhne, to take me away tonight, to stay at my side and to keep me from Finn.'

With those words, Diarmuid's life changed course.

'So be it,' said Diarmuid, who would not break any bonds a woman placed upon him; for to do so would make him a man without honour. 'Put on a cloak, fill a bag with food and meet me at the lowest part of the western wall.'

So Grainne left, and Diarmuid went to his closest friends and tried to wake them. Only Ossian, Caoilte, and Oscar awoke, for they had not drunk deeply of the mead. Diarmuid told them what had happened and asked their advice.

'If bonds have been put on you then you must go,' said Ossian. 'Though I will be sore to lose you.'

'Go,' said Caoilte. 'You must dishonour yourself either way, and this is the lesser dishonour.'

'You must go,' said Oscar, 'and know that you go with our love.'

Diarmuid had hoped for a way out, something he had not seen; but they gave him none. So he filled a pack, stuffing it with loaves of bread from the kitchens, and went to meet Grainne at the foot of the west wall.

'We should not do this,' he said to her. 'Forget your love; think of your name, and mine, and that of Finn.'

'We will do this, and I will make you glad we did,' said Grainne, leaning forward to kiss him. Diarmuid backed away. 'I will not break my faith with Finn,' he said. 'I will leave unbroken bread everywhere we stop to prove it.'

Grainne's face fell. 'Come on,' she said. 'We need to get away before the sun rises.'

'I am under bonds never to go through any side door,' said Diarmuid. He walked a few paces back, ran at the wall and used his spear to vault over the top of it.

Grainne met him on the other side, and they made their escape.

THE WOOD
OF TWO HUTS

In the fields beneath the hill they found a horse tethered. They rode it north-west to the banks of the Shannon. At the ford named Ath-Luain, they left the horse behind, fearing its hoof prints would betray them. Into the river itself they went next, thinking to throw off Finn's hounds as they waded upstream. Finally, they struck west into the province of Connacht.

Diarmuid led Grainne to a forest where he and Finn had once hunted. Its name was Doire-da-Bhoth, the Wood of Two Huts, for deep within it was a pair of huts used by hunters. As the first half-light of dawn seeped through the trees, they saw the huts before them.

'You take that hut,' said Diarmuid. 'I will take this one.'

'I would rather we shared a hut,' said Grainne.

'I would rather be back at Allen,' said Diarmuid.

Grainne went sullenly into her hut. Diarmuid did not rest; he took his hand axe and set to building a fence. Finn would not be far behind them.

When Finn awakened earlier that night, he soon learnt that Diarmuid and Grainne were missing.

Could it be? Could his friend through so many adventures have stolen his bride, when Finn had charged him with guarding her?

Of course. Finn had feared that he was too old for Grainne. His men had laughed at him and desired her for themselves. He had watched her during the feast, watched how she looked at the younger men.

Finn brought himself back to the present. All his men were gathered in the hall, waiting for his words.

'Arm yourselves,' said Finn as Bran whined at his feet. 'We are going hunting.'

Soon after that, the whole force of the Fianna poured out of the gates. Their hounds found the scent and followed it all the way to the Shannon. The stolen horse grazed there by the bank, but the trail vanished.

'Take the hounds to the far bank,' said Finn to his best scouts. 'Move up and downriver until you find the scent.' They did as commanded, yet for a long the time the trail was not found.

In his mind, Finn saw Diarmuid laughing at him. He grabbed a passing man. 'Tell those scouts that if the trail is not found before noon, I will hang every one of them.' The man's eyes bulged, he nodded and ran off.

Soon afterwards, the trail was found, and the Fianna moved west into Connacht. Finn grinned; he knew where Diarmuid was heading.

'Diarmuid has taken her to the Wood of Two Huts,' he said to Ossian, who ran beside him. 'Two of them went in; only one shall leave.'

Ossian was worried. Feigning tiredness, he fell back to run beside his son Oscar.

'I fear what will come of this,' he said. 'I fear what is happening in my father's heart. We must warn Diarmuid, yet we have no way to reach him.'

'Send Bran ahead,' suggested Oscar. 'She loves Diarmuid almost as much as she loves Finn, and will want not want Finn to see out this evil.'

Ossian agreed and ran ahead to catch up with Bran, bending down to whisper in her ear. Finn's hound licked his hand and raced

ahead, surging through the long grass until she reached the Wood
of the Two Huts. She found Diarmuid and laid her head in his lap.

Grainne emerged from her hut.

'I recognise that hound,' said Grainne, her face turning pale.
'That … that is Finn's hound.'

'Yes,' said Diarmuid. 'This is Bran.'

'Finn has found us?'

'I think so,' said Diarmuid. 'I think Bran has come to warn us
that Finn is on his way.'

'We need to go then!'

Diarmuid shook his head, stroking Bran, a sad smile upon his lips.

'No. We will face Finn here, and I will tell him the truth of what
happened.' He looked at Grainne. 'I will have him know that if I
betrayed him, I did not do so willingly.'

Grainne did not reply, but went back into her hut, full of anger
and fear.

❧

It was evening when the Fianna arrived at the wood.

'This makes no sense,' said Ossian to his father. 'Diarmuid would
not stop here in a place where the two of you have hunted before.'

Fin stepped closer to Ossian.

'If Diarmuid did not stop here,' said Finn, 'it is because you sent
Bran ahead to warn him.'

Ossian tried to form a reply, but Finn gave him a dark look and
turned away. 'Into the woods,' he told his men.

Calling their hounds close, the Fianna stalked through the trees
until they saw before them a tall fence. Walking around it, they saw
that it had seven doors and was newly built. The barking of the hounds
became deafening, and Finn knew that he had his prey trapped.

'Put men at every door,' he said to Lugaidh, who was one of his
most trusted men.

❧

'Grandfather,' said Oscar, growing desperate. 'I am sure we are in the wrong place. Diarmuid wouldn't allow himself to be surrounded. If we leave this place behind, we will surely find him.'

'Do not take me for a fool, Oscar,' said Finn. 'Diarmuid!' he shouted. 'I know you are in there, whatever your friends here may say. You have my bride. Give her back.'

The warriors waited, listening, and then heard Diarmuid reply.

'Yes, Finn, I'm here,' he called out. 'And I have Grainne with me. She put me under bonds to take her away, and you know well that I could not do otherwise.'

'You could have remembered your bond to me,' said Finn. 'To your captain and friend. But a pretty face made you forget all that and reveal your true nature. Open one of these doors, give Grainne to me and I will consider mercy.'

What no one there knew was that far away, another one who loved Diarmuid was surveying this scene. Angus Og, Bright Warrior of the Sun, had been woken by visions of Diarmuid. When he looked into the flames of his fire he saw Diarmuid, who had once been his foster son, and saw all that had happened. Swiftly he left his hall of Bru-Na-Boinne and summoned a druid wind to carry him over the country. Using his cloak of invisibility, he flew over Ireland, over the fence and to Diarmuid's side.

'If you were ever in trouble, lad, you are in trouble now,' murmured Angus. 'Come under my cloak and I will take you both away from here.'

Diarmuid shook his head. 'Take Grainne. I will not walk away from this.'

'Don't be stupid!' hissed Grainne. 'Finn has all the Fianna surrounding us. You won't make it out of here alive.'

'Whether I do, or don't, I will not leave now,' said Diarmuid. Knowing he would not be swayed, Angus took Grainne beneath his cloak and carried her over the fence and away.

Darkness had come. Myriad torches brightened the night.

Diarmuid moved to the nearest door. He said in a low voice, 'Who stands at this door?'

'No enemy of yours,' came the answer. 'Here stands Ossian, and Oscar, and our kinsmen. We will not fight you, but will help you escape.'

Diarmuid moved on, for he wished to talk with Finn.

'Who stands at this door?'

'Caoilte, and the sons of Ronan,' came the answer. 'Come out, Diarmuid, and we will vouch for you with Finn.' But Diarmuid moved on.

'Who stands at this door?'

'Goll,' came the reply, 'and all the Sons of Morna. We have no love for Finn. If you wish to take his place and take his wife as your own, you need only side with us, and we will see it done.'

So Diarmuid had his fears of Goll's treachery confirmed, and moved on.

He learnt at the fourth door, and again at the fifth, that many of the Fianna had disloyalty in their hearts. They envied Finn and desired power for themselves.

'Who stand at this door?' he asked at the sixth door.

'Aodh Fada of Eamhuin and all his men. We are no friends of yours, Diarmuid O'Duibhne.' Diarmuid was heartened by that, for the treachery he had discovered sickened him.

He came to the last door.

'Who stands there?' he asked.

'Finn MacCoull,' was the answer. 'Come for you, oath breaker.'

'I did not ask for this, Finn,' said Diarmuid. 'But here we stand; so I will tell you that you will not take me prisoner, nor will you profit from chasing me. Your men turn against you even as we speak, and I fear the Fianna will fall if we let this rift between us deepen. Let me go, take another wife, and forget Grainne.'

'Your silken tongue may have won you my wife, but it will not win me,' said Finn. 'Draw your sword, Diarmuid.'

Finn drew back. 'Make a ram!' he shouted to his men. 'Bring down this door.'

They did as he ordered, shattering the door.

Finn stepped through it and found Diarmuid gone. He had made the salmon leap with the aid of his spears, leaping unseen over the heads of the Fianna while they worked. Across the country he ran, until he came to the hut where Angus and Grainne were waiting for him.

Finn searched the huts, and found nothing but a loaf of unbroken bread.

With Angus watching over them, Diarmuid and Grainne at last slept. The next morning, after they had eaten, Angus spoke to them over the flickering fire.

'It is a hard road you two shall walk,' he said. 'And a dark path Finn's mind has taken. The Son of Coull will not rest in his pursuit; there is no tool he will not use to find you. Move quickly. Where you hunt, do not cook; where you cook, do not eat; where you eat, do not sleep. Do not stop on an island with only one harbour; do not enter a cave with only one mouth.'

With those word Angus left Diarmuid and Grainne, who soon set off into the wet, misty morning. They left behind them a loaf of unbroken bread, and they knew not what lay ahead of them.

THE GREEN CHAMPIONS

As rain fell and mist rolled across the country, Diarmuid and Grainne travelled west to the bog of Fionnliath, where it would be hard for Finn to hunt them.

They stopped in the afternoon. Diarmuid made a fire, judging that they had evaded any pursuit for now. As they sat warming themselves among the mud and rushes, there emerged out of the fog the shape of a man.

Diarmuid leapt to his feet and drew his sword, yet did not strike. The man was young and strong, but was not of the Fianna, and had a gentle look about him.

'Who are you?' asked Diarmuid.

'My name is Muadhan,' said the young man. 'I am a hunter, and I wish to be a fighting man, so I am in search of a master.'

'You should take him into your service,' murmured Grainne. 'He could be of help to us.'

'I am a fighting man,' said Diarmuid, 'and I could use a servant.'

So Diarmuid and Muadhan bound themselves to one another, and Diarmuid charged Muadhan with providing supper. He did so, spearing a salmon in the next river they came to. Mindful of Angus' advice, they crossed the river and went into the woods to cook it.

'You may divide the fish,' said Diarmuid to Muadhan, for to do so was an honour and he was grateful for Muadhan's service.

'In that case, I shall give Diarmuid the biggest portion, and give Grainne the second biggest, and take for myself the smallest,' said Muadhan, smiling. 'For if Diarmuid had divided the fish, he would have given the biggest portion to Grainne, and if Grainne had divided the fish, she would have given the biggest portion to Diarmuid.'

After eating they moved onwards, finding another place to sleep. In the morning they walked awhile before sharing some bread. They moved across the country, always taking a different direction, wary and watchful for any pursuit.

In this time, Diarmuid began to feel more at ease with Grainne, and to cling less to the anger he felt towards her. He would have expected the High King's Daughter to complain about the weather, the walking and the beds of hard earth; yet she complained not once. Grainne was indeed cold, tired and sore, but being beside Diarmuid made her happy. She only wished he would show her more affection than he did.

One day they came to a cave near the western sea. They made their beds within and decided that, since it was days since they had seen any sign of pursuit, it would be safe to rest there awhile and let Grainne regain her strength. Muadhan caught and cooked their supper again, and afterwards Grainne sang for them both, a long song from when the world was young.

The night passed. Diarmuid awoke first. His senses told him all was not well. He woke Muadhan, ordered him in a whisper to stay and guard Grainne, and left. Running across country and uphill to the nearest vantage point, Diarmuid looked out to sea and felt a fire in his heart go out.

'No, Finn,' he said. 'You have not. You would not.'

For docked in the harbour below were ships carrying the flags of the Green Champions.

'Mercenaries,' said Diarmuid. 'Murderers.'

Diarmuid had never met one of their number, but tales were told of the green warriors in every mead hall between west and east. They went from country to country taking what they wanted, be that men, women, children or gold. They were fighters for hire, of no small skill, yet honour and heroism in battle meant nothing to them.

Never since Finn took his captaincy had they dared raid Ireland's shores. Was it a coincidence that they came now – or had they been hired? Surely Finn would not stoop to this?

Diarmuid would have to find out.

Diarmuid walked out of the forest that bordered the Green Champions' camp. He sauntered up to the sentries and asked to speak to their leaders. So fearless was he that they allowed him through, and now he found himself stood before three heavily armed and jewel-laden men.

'It is a rare man who comes walking towards these banners,' said one of them. 'What makes you think you will walk away from them?'

'A man must walk somewhere,' said Diarmuid. 'Why not towards men of bravery and strength? Especially when he has them himself.'

'You hold yourself in high regard,' said another of the three.

'I have reason to,' said Diarmuid. 'I am a wandering warrior, and I have not met a man of my worth between earth and sky.'

'Perhaps that's true,' said the third man. 'Or perhaps my men will cut you open and eat your liver for breakfast.'

'Perhaps,' said Diarmuid. 'But then you would miss out on seeing my tricks.'

'What tricks?' said the first man, who was fond of tricks.

'Bring me an empty ale barrel and I'll show you.'

So a barrel was brought and unstoppered, and Diarmuid and the three Captains of the Green Champions drank together. Their names were Fairfoot, Blackfoot and Strongfoot. Once the barrel

was empty, Diarmuid leapt up on to it and ran upon it, all the way up the nearest hill and all the way back down again, leaping off with a flourish.

'Ha!' laughed a green-clad warrior nearby. 'It is a man who has never seen tricks, who calls that a trick.'

'Do it better then,' said Diarmuid. The man leapt onto the barrel, ran up the hill on it and down again. As it rolled past him, Diarmuid surreptitiously kicked the barrel, which fell on the man and flattened him.

'I'll try that!' said another warrior. The same thing happened. Another tried, and in this way Diarmuid disposed of dozens of the Green Champions before taking his leave.

The next morning Diarmuid came into the camp again.

'What are you wanting?' asked Fairfoot.

'To join the Green Champions,' said Diarmuid.

'If you want to join us, you'll need to earn your place,' said Strong-foot. 'We seek Diarmuid, and news of him is what we value; for Finn MacCoull has offered half his riches if we bring Diarmuid to him.'

'I met a man the other day who said he knew Diarmuid. I will go looking for him. In the meantime, would you care to see a trick?'

The mercenaries said yes, they would like to see a trick. So Diarmuid took his spear, stuck the hilt into the soil so that it stood upright, and leapt into the air. He landed upon his spear tip, spinning and contorting there so that the Champions laughed and cheered.

'It is a man who has never seen feats, who calls that a feat!' said a warrior as Diarmuid finished.

He elbowed his way forward, his companions cheering him on. The man leapt upon the spear and was skewered as if he were meat for the fire.

'Let me try!' said another, after the first man was removed. He met the same fate, as did the man after him, and the man after him, and the man after him. It went on until evening, until heaps of men lay dead, and Diarmuid bid them goodnight.

The next morning, he walked into their camp again.

'You!' said Blackfoot. 'Did you speak to your man? Do you have news of Diarmuid?'

'Tomorrow,' said Diarmuid. 'He said he'll have the news for me tomorrow, and I'll surely share it with you then, if you'll let me join.'

'We'll see,' said Fairfoot.

'Good,' said Diarmuid. 'But today must pass before tomorrow comes. Would you like to see a trick?'

Diarmuid dug two wooden poles into the earth. He lay his sword between them with the blade facing upwards. He leapt on to it and walked back and forth.

'It is a man who has never seen tricks, who calls that a trick!' came the now familiar cry.

The Green Champions tried one by one to copy Diarmuid. Every warrior who did so was cut in half.

'Goodnight,' said Diarmuid, as the sun began to set. 'I'll bring news of Diarmuid tomorrow.'

'Just as well,' said Blackfoot. 'We've lost enough men to you and your tricks.'

Diarmuid returned to the cave and ate his supper with Muadhan and Grainne.

Come morning, he returned the Green Champions' camp.

As he approached, he sensed a change in the air. Men stood as they saw him, put their hands on their sword hilts and curled their lips.

'You said you would bring news of Diarmuid today,' said Fairfoot. 'I did.'

'Give it to us then.'

'You don't want to see a trick?'

'You've played enough tricks on us already, Diarmuid O'Duibhne,' said Strongfoot.

Diarmuid grinned and drew his sword. 'That I have.'

The three Captains roared and threw themselves at Diarmuid. They were fearsome fighters. The Captains worked as one, surrounding Diarmuid and creating openings for one another. Yet as fierce and skilled as they were, Diarmuid had learnt swordplay from Angus, and fought beside Finn. He had defeated an entire army in the realm beneath the waves.

The Captains soon tired. Diarmuid took advantage of their every mistake. He forced them back, knocked their weapons from their hands and soon had them on their backs. They bled from many wounds; their eyes were wide with fear.

'Do not expect us to beg,' said Blackfoot.

Diarmuid ignored him. He walked over to a tent and emerged with a length of rope in his hand. When the men saw their Captains fall, they had all run for their ships. Now they watched from the prows as Diarmuid bound their leaders, using knots known only to a few of the Fianna. Should any man try to release the Captains, other than Caoilte, Ossian or Oscar, the nets would only hold them tighter.

Diarmuid once more went home to the cave. He told Grainne and Muadhan how he had bound the leaders of the Green Champions.

'Then we are safe to remain here?' asked Grainne.

'No,' said Diarmuid. 'The Champions have seen me, and we are too near to them. If we stay here, either the Champions or Finn will find us.'

Grainne was saddened. It had been a relief to bide in one place for a while. Diarmuid had not seemed angry at her these last few days, his fury instead focussed on the mercenaries staining Ireland's shore. They slept one more night in the cave before putting out the fire and moving on, leaving behind them unbroken bread.

Back through the bog of Fionnliath they went, hoping that their trail would be lost there if hounds were sent after them. Afterwards they turned towards the hills of Slieve Luachra. Up through the rain-soaked glens they went, until they found another cave and made a new home there.

Back at the Green Champions' camp, the men had left the ships and gathered around their Captains. One by one and in two and threes they laboured to undo Diarmuid's knots. They succeeded only in binding their leaders tighter, until the Captains' flesh was purple and swollen and they swore at their men to stop.

Food was fed to the Captains through the ropes. Drink was poured into their mouths. The men sat by their fires, wondering what to do next. This was the way of things when a black-clad woman approached their camp.

'Who are you?' asked a scarred, brown-bearded warrior, the next in command after the three Captains.

'The Woman of the Black Mountain,' she answered. 'I am scouring the country on behalf of Finn, who will richly reward anyone with news of Diarmuid O'Duibhne.'

'Oh, we can give you news of Diarmuid O'Duibhne,' said Blackfoot from within his bonds. He told her all that had happened.

'Fools,' she said.

The Woman of the Black Mountain turned toward the forest and spoke the words of a spell. Thunder rumbled in the sky and the Champions shivered, clutching at whatever charms they carried.

From out of the forest came three hounds. They were the size of horses, black and terrible, with flaming red eyes and slavering jaws. The Champions drew back as the hounds stalked towards their master, nuzzled her and sniffed at the Captains in their bonds. Their growling was like the splitting of mountains.

'Not them, my dears,' said the woman. 'They are not your prey.' She turned to the scarred warrior. 'Do you have anything belonging to Diarmuid?'

'No,' said the warrior, 'but I can show you what way he went when he left our camp.'

'Show me.'

He did, and moments later the hounds were howling; they had Diarmuid's scent.

'Diarmuid is mine now,' said the woman.

'If you find him first,' said the scarred warrior.

The woman laughed. 'Yes,' she said. 'If I find him first'.

She turned and ran after her hounds, faster than a diving hawk.

Diarmuid, Grainne and Muadhan were at home in their cave. Muadhan had proved his usefulness once again, catching a fat and juicy trout. All three of them were feeling rested from the journey, the deep cold of the marshes finally leaving their bones. Grainne and Muadhan both treated Diarmuid's wounds, and Grainne entertained them with her songs.

The next morning, Grainne awoke and looked at Diarmuid. He opened his eyes and smiled at her.

'May I borrow your knife,' she said, 'to cut my nails?'

Diarmuid nodded and took his knife from where he kept it on his belt, even in sleep. Grainne set to cutting her nails as Muadhan yawned, stretched and rose to awaken the fire. He blew upon it, walked to the cave mouth and roared, 'Up! Up!'

Diarmuid and Grainne sprang up and ran to the cave mouth. Racing up the glen were three dogs the size of horses, a black-clad woman not far behind them.

The dogs saw them watching and howled. The woman laughed. They had their prey trapped.

'"Do not enter a cave with only one mouth,"' said Diarmuid, quoting Angus. 'I'm a fool and it will be the death of us.'

'We could –' began Grainne, but Diarmuid interrupted her.

'Give me my knife!' he grabbed it from her. 'I was a fool long before today. I was a fool to ever give any man my friend-ship.' Grainne was hurt by his words and frightened by his fear. 'Muadhan, take her into the rear of the cave. Go as far as you can.'

'I can help –'

'Go!' said Diarmuid. Muadhan took her hand and led her into the darkness that soon swallowed them.

Diarmuid turned back to the hounds.

They were almost at the cave mouth. The gully leading to the cave was narrow, meaning they could only approach one at a time. At the bottom of the glen, Diarmuid saw a group of the Green Champions, led by a scarred, brown-bearded man.

Diarmuid drew his spears.

The first hound reached the narrow gully. It bounded towards Diarmuid as he released his first spear. The Red Spear buried itself in the hound's shoulder, yet the hound kept coming.

It leapt into the cave. It was almost upon him.

The hound leapt at Diarmuid. He waited until its jaws were wide open; then he threw the Yellow Spear into its mouth. The hound came crashing down.

Before Diarmuid could retrieve his spear, the second hound leapt over the body of its brother.

Diarmuid edged back as the hound stalked towards him, towering over him.

His hand went to his sword hilt. The hound watched, mockery in its eyes. What it did not notice was that the Yellow Spear was attached to Diarmuid's hand by a length of cord.

He pulled on the cord. The spear leapt back into his hand.

Enraged, the hound leapt at it him. It met the same fate as the first.

The third hound entered the cave and climbed over the bodies of its brothers.

Diarmuid pulled on his spear string. This one was too quick. It leapt on the cord, bit down and severed it.

The hound moved towards Diarmuid.

His sword raised, Diarmuid watched the beast draw closer. Its red eyes pulled him in, telling him to cease fighting and give himself up to death.

Then a strange thing happened.

He heard footsteps behind him; the heavy tread of Muadhan. A tiny pup darted between Diarmuid's legs.

The hound snarled at it. The pup snarled back, ran at the hound and leapt at it, right into its jaws.

The hound gave out a ghastly howl of pain. It fell writhing to the floor, slavering and moaning, jerking and thrashing. It finally fell still as the pup squeezed itself out of the hound's rear, covered in blood and wagging its tail.

Diarmuid's jaw hung open as he watched the pup lick its lips, turn around and trot back towards Muadhan. The young fighting man patted its head, tickled its chin and held open a leather pouch. The pup hopped inside. Muadhan tied the pouch and put it upon his belt.

'The Green Champions,' he said to Diarmuid.

Diarmuid recovered himself. With Muadhan at his side, he walked out of the cave and down the gully to meet the mercenaries. Side by side and back to back, they made corpses of their enemies. When the fighting was done, they burned the bodies so that Slieve Luachra would be cleansed of the stain.

ᘓᘏᘐ

The Woman of the Black Mountain watched the battle from a hiding place. Seeing her hounds and the Green Champions defeated, she turned and ran, all the way to the hall upon the Hill of Allen, and gave her report to Finn.

Finn did not wait. He gathered a force of men and they crossed the country to the Champions' camp. The dying Captains lay in their bonds, starving, filthy and wretched.

'Release us, Finn,' said Fairfoot. But Finn could not. The bonds Diarmuid had made could only be loosened by Caoilte, Ossian or Oscar. Of them, only Ossian was present.

'Release them, Ossian,' said Finn.

'I will not release such men,' said Ossian. 'This is the fate they have given to others. It is the fate they deserve.'

'I am your father and Captain,' said Finn. 'You will release them.'

'I will not.'

Finn stared at his son, each of them full of sadness and anger.

Every man present tensed himself, ready to take a side and to strike.

Finn turned away from Ossian. 'If a son such as you, who dishonours his father, can loosen these bonds, then I surely can,' he said.

He walked over to the bound Captains and bent down to begin work on their bonds; but they were already dead.

No man spoke on the way back to Allen.

ᘓᘏᘐ

THE BERRY TREE

Diarmuid, Grainne and Muadhan trudged onwards.

Their encounter with the hounds had left them heavy-hearted. The weather was against them, and Grainne still smarted from Diarmuid's words within the cave. It seemed that any affection he felt for her could vanish with the wind.

Avoiding Diarmuid's eye, she would have taken comfort in Muadhan's presence. Come rain or cold, he was always at ease; yet even Muadhan seemed distant.

At camp the next morning, before the sun had risen, Muadhan said, 'I am leaving now. It has been an honour to serve you, Diarmuid; that service is at an end.'

Diarmuid spluttered and argued and came as close to pleading as pride would allow him. Muadhan would not be dissuaded. He wished them both luck and melted into the mist.

'I am sorry you have lost Muadhan,' said Grainne.

'So am I,' said Diarmuid. 'But we shall manage well enough.'

Grainne smiled at that. They packed up their camp and left behind them a loaf of unbroken bread.

෴

They walked north for many days, never stopping for long, for Finn was on their tail again. Many were the spies he sent searching for them, and many were the nights that Grainne awoke from nightmares of red-eyed hounds. She would look at Diarmuid in the firelight, always sleeping some way from her, and despite all she had suffered, she was happy.

෴

At length they came to the Wood of Dubhros, the Dark Forest, in Connacht. Crossing a farmer's fields one moonlit evening, Diarmuid saw the wood ahead and said to Grainne, 'We can stop here tonight.'

They moved among the trees, Grainne now used to finding her way through the darkness. A little way in, they made a fire and made camp for the night. Grainne asked Diarmuid if he knew anything of this place.

'No,' said Diarmuid, inspecting his fingernails.

He had heard a story about this wood, though he did not know if anything lay behind it.

It was said that in years past, two women of the Tuatha De Danaan loved two men. One man was of their own race; one was of the Fianna. The women got to arguing over which man was the better hurler, and this turned into an argument over which race were better hurlers. So a contest was arranged, somewhere in Connacht, and on his way home from the contest, a man of the Tuatha De Danaan dropped a berry from his pocket.

There grew in that spot a fairy tree, huge and dripping with berries that could be found nowhere else in Ireland. It was said that the berries tasted finer than starlight and gave those who ate them bliss, health and long life.

The elders of the Children of Danu discovered the tree and sought out the man who dropped the berry. Finding him, they ordered him to guard the tree and ensure no mortal touched them. Such food was only for their own kind.

The man didn't want to spend the rest of his life guarding a tree. After some thought, he went to the tree, took a fistful of berries and travelled over the western sea, until he came to an island where the Fomorians dwelt. There, he searched for one who would be willing to guard the tree, in exchange for all the berries they could ever hope to eat.

Deep within a cave, he met a one-eyed giant called the Surly One. The Surly One tasted the berries and agreed at once to guard the tree.

He crossed the sea to Ireland and made his home beneath the tree; or that, at least, was what the story said. If all this were true, the giant was somewhere deep within the wood. Whether it were true or not – and this was what interested Diarmuid – the fear of the Surly One kept travellers away from the forest.

Perhaps they could be safe here.

Diarmuid woke before dawn and left Grainne sleeping. He went deeper into the wood, treading softly. Deeper still he went, the forest growing thicker about him, until he came to a place where no birds sang and no spiders spun webs.

His footsteps seemed as loud as the ringing of iron. Diarmuid walked on, sweat breaking out on his brow. There was something in the air of this place that made his head swim.

Finally Diarmuid stopped.

He had found the Surly One.

The giant sat with his back to the trunk of the mightiest tree Diarmuid had ever seen. Its branches danced like a multitude of serpents and its shimmering leaves were every colour of the rainbow. The tree sang to Diarmuid, its chorus of ethereal voices inviting him to taste the forbidden fruit that hung down in fat, purple clumps.

'I wouldn't do that if I were you,' said the Fomorian.

'Do what?'

'Try for a berry or two from the tree. Because these berries are mine,' said the Surly One, 'and anyone who tries to steal them gets their head squashed like a berry.' He picked up a club that lay at his side, which was itself as thick as a hundred year-old oak, and waved it at Diarmuid.

'You don't know me,' said Diarmuid, 'so you don't know what my word is worth. But I swear to you that I have no interest in your berries.'

'Is that so?' said the Surly One with a chuckle. 'What brought you here, then, if it was not to steal from me?'

So Diarmuid sat and told the giant his tale. The Surly One was enthralled. He had not heard a story for many years. Few people came to the Dark Wood, and he was quick to smash the skull of any who did so.

When Diarmuid had finished, the Surly One said, 'I liked your story. I would like to hear more. You can stay in my woods, as long as you come by now and then to tell me stories, and don't try to steal my berries.'

And to that, Diarmuid happily agreed.

※

While Diarmuid and Grainne built a cabin, Finn brooded.

The Fianna no longer feasted together in the evenings. Instead they ate in small groups, throwing distrustful glances towards men sat at other tables. They might not have come to Allen at all, except Finn demanded that they show loyalty to him by showing face. He sat alone, watching his men or gazing darkly into the distance.

On one such evening, two men whom Finn had not seen before were brought before him by Ossian.

'Angus, son of Art Og, is my name,' said the first.

'Aodh, son of Andela, is mine,' said the second.

They explained their business. Both of them were of Clan Morna. Their fathers had fought against Coull, Finn's father, the day he was slain. They were raised by their mothers and now wished to join the Fianna.

'Though our fathers were enemies,' said Aodh, 'We wish to be friends and servants of the Son of Coull.'

Their words were met with silence from Finn.

Finn had recently found himself thinking of his father. He had never met his father, the mighty Coull, whom Goll MacMorna

had slain. Goll had made peace with Finn years ago and the Sons
of Morna had remained among the Fianna. But in recent days,
as Finn looked about his hall, he had wondered why he must be
allied with the butchers of his father. Could he cast them out?
The Fianna could surely afford to lose a few men. But he had
made his peace with Goll. So Finn's mind would circle.

'It occurs to me,' said Finn at last, 'that I never claimed any
blood price for my father's death. I was young, I suppose, when I
took my captaincy. Over-eager to be accepted. Maybe the time has
come to claim that price.'

'A blood price cannot be claimed for a man killed in battle, as
well you know,' said Ossian, looking at his father with barely disguised disgust.

'If I were to be killed, any peasant in his hut could afford
the blood price you would demand,' hissed Finn, returning
Ossian's look.

He turned back to Angus and Aodh. 'You may have my forgiveness, and the freedom to take the trials of the Fianna,' said Finn.
'Providing you bring me either of two things.

'There is a tale that speaks of a magical tree in the Wood of
Dubhros in Connacht. Bring me some berries from the tree, which
they say is guarded by a fearsome Fomorian.'

'Or?' asked Angus.

Finn smiled, and his smile was empty of joy. 'Or bring me
Diarmuid O'Duibhne's head.'

The hut in the Dark Wood was built. Diarmuid and Grainne
carved a table and chairs, bowls and cups to make of it a home.
The hunting was good, for no other hunter dared step beneath
those boughs. Each evening, they shared their food before sitting
back to share stories, riddles and songs.

Diarmuid taught Grainne to carve; Grainne taught Diarmuid to sing. When they ran out of songs, they made up their own. Laughter often poured through the woods as beneath the berry tree the Surly One slept.

Of the tree and its berries, Diarmuid said nothing to Grainne. He merely told her to keep away from that part of the wood.

Diarmuid still kept his faith with Finn. It cost him many a sleepless night, for day by day, Grainne was winning his heart. He would lie awake, watching the flame-light caress her, and write songs in his mind that he never dared to share with her. As for Grainne, she asked for nothing more than she got from him, for his refusals hurt too much for her to bear. So a winter passed in which they grew closer and closer, yet never touched.

Early one spring morning, they were awoken by a thudding on the door. Diarmuid had taken care to build it low so that no enemy could burst through. Though they been undisturbed for so long, they kept it bolted every night.

Sword in hand, Diarmuid approached the door, while Grainne rose and took hold of a knife.

'Who knocks at our door?' asked Diarmuid.

'Angus and Aodh,' came the answer. 'We came seeking the berries of the Wood of Dubhros, that give those who eat them pleasure, health and long life. But finding this hut, so deep in such a forest, we wonder who dwells in it.'

'A woodsman and his wife,' said Diarmuid to the door.

'Show yourself to us then,' said Angus. 'Otherwise we will have cause to think that it is Diarmuid and Grainne who hide in this hut.'

'I need not show my face to you,' said Diarmuid.

Outside, Angus and Aodh chuckled. 'You are clever, Diarmuid O'Duibhne. Finn gave us a choice; bring us the berries or your head. We scoured the country all winter, thinking your head would be an easier prize than to take on the Fomorian.

'We gave up and came here for the berries, only to find you here where none would think to look. So come out now and fight, or we will cut down the door, or smoke you out.'

'I could come out and fight you,' said Diarmuid, 'and you would be rare men indeed if you won. But I ask you, why do this? Why serve Finn? I know the man whom you think he is; the wise, generous hero of a thousand tales. He was that man once, but is no longer. Jealousy and hatred have turned him into –'

'Shame on you!' cried Aodh. 'Is it not enough that you steal his wife, at his wedding, when he has charged you with guarding her; must you insult him too?'

Diarmuid rested his brow against the door. 'So be it,' he said. 'Blood shall be spilt.'

Yet no blood was spilt. He went out and met the young men in combat; they showed no great skill. Sporting not even a bruise, Diarmuid soon had them prone upon the forest floor.

'I could kill you both,' he said as Grainne looked on. 'If I do not, you will go back to Finn and tell him we are here. We shall be forced to move again and make the wet earth our bed. Yet it would be the slaughtering of pups, not the fair killing of combat, and would stain my hands.'

'Let us go then,' said Angus, 'and we will swear not to tell Finn you are here.'

'So you would be dishonest?'

'Yes.'

'Then how can I accept your oath?' Diarmuid rolled his eyes. 'I see no easy way out of this.'

'I see a way,' said Grainne.

'What way is that?' asked Diarmuid.

'Go to the tree,' she said. 'This tree that you never saw fit to mention before. Take the berries from it, and give them to these men, and let them take the berries to Finn. He will be so pleased with his prize – a glorious food that confers joy and health and long life – that he will not be thinking of you.'

'It is a good plan,' said Diarmuid, 'but for one thing. I promised the Surly One I would not try to take his berries.'

'Well, how about this,' said Grainne. 'I am angry that you kept a secret from me. I want to taste those berries, and if you do not bring me them, I will go there and take on this Surly One myself.'

'You don't mean it,' said Diarmuid.

'I do,' said Grainne.

Once more Diarmuid found himself beneath the berry tree. He had kept his word to the Surly One and came often to tell him stories.

'Diarmuid!' said the Surly One. 'Come and sit down. I've been thinking about the story of Ossian and his mother. Would you tell it to me again?'

'No,' said Diarmuid. 'I'm not here to tell stories.'

Grainne, Angus and Aodh approached and stopped behind Diarmuid, staring up at the giant. The young men had pleaded to watch the fight, and Diarmuid had thought it mean to refuse them.

'I do not like the look in your eyes,' said the Surly One.

He stood, reached out and snatched a handful of berries from the tree.

'I do not like that you have come here armed,' he said as he filled his mouth with berries, juices dripping down his chin. 'And I do not like that you have come here in company.'

'I do not like that I am here either,' said Diarmuid. 'For you have treated me kindly and fairly. But I am here, and I have come for the berries. Give me a few handfuls, and you will live to see the sunset.'

The Surly One narrowed his eye, curled his lip and took his club from where it lay by the tree.

No more words were spoken.

The giant roared and ran at Diarmuid, swinging his club overhead. Diarmuid leapt out of the way as the club smashed down, shaking the ground. Grainne, Angus and Aodh were knocked off their feet.

The Surly One growled. He pulled his club from the crater he had made and swung it again. Diarmuid ducked and dodged as the club swung back and forth, whistling through the air and pounding the ground. The Surly One roared and cursed as the onlookers ran for cover.

Back and forth across the clearing the combatants moved. The great leaps needed to stay ahead of the club were tiring Diarmuid, yet the Surly One, his stomach full of berries, was as fresh as the spring rain. He laughed as he saw Diarmuid slowing.

'Soon, now, false friend,' he said. 'Soon I will wash down my berries with your blood.'

'I will have the berries,' said Diarmuid, 'and after I taste them, I shall cut down your tree.'

'You … you would not …'

The Surly One lost all control. He swung wildly as a mist of rage fell on him.

The club buried itself in the ground before Diarmuid, who took his chance. Diarmuid leapt up on to the club, ran up the Surly One's arm and shoulder and on to his head.

'I will cut up your tree, and burn it on my fireplace, on warm days when I have no need of a fire,' said Diarmuid into the Fomorian's ear.

It was too much. The Surly One pulled his club out of the ground and brought it smashing down on his own head.

Diarmuid leapt away into the branches of the tree. He watched as the giant clubbed himself three times upon the head before falling dead upon the forest floor.

The onlookers cheered. They rushed forward to climb the tree and taste its fruit.

Diarmuid sat and looked sadly upon the body of his friend.

༄

Finn held out his hand. Into it, Angus dropped the berries.

Finn put his hand to his lips, sniffed the berries and frowned.

'So you would earn your place among the Fianna by deceiving me?' he asked.

'Deceiving you? There is no –'

'There is a smell upon these berries,' said Finn. 'One I know well. It is the scent of Diarmuid O'Duibhne.'

'I …' So afraid was Angus that he could not finish the lie.

'I could give you death or silver,' said Finn. 'For you have lied to me, and yet you have told me where Diarmuid is, and my wife with him. Her scent I never got the chance to know.'

He turned to the nearest man watching. 'Fortunately for them, I do not kill boys. Unfortunately for them, I do not reward them either. Ready the Fianna.'

With that, Angus and Aodh were dismissed, as the Fianna prepared to hunt Diarmuid once more.

༄

By the last light of a spring evening, Finn, his men and their hounds entered the Dark Wood. They found the cabin. It lay empty. Following Diarmuid's scent, they entered the deep forest.

As the shadows lengthened and the light grew dim, the warriors began to whisper and to point at a strange sight.

There was a patch of forest ahead that was lit up as if the sun rested there. Forward they moved, Finn at their head, coming to a halt before the berry tree.

༄

There was no night in that place. The tree gave off its own light, every leaf illuminating its neighbours with shimmering, incandescent light. Every colour to be found beneath the sky was reflected in the eyes of the men who stood, open-mouthed, beneath the dancing, shimmering leaves.

Finn followed his hounds to the base of the tree and looked up.

'Diarmuid is in this tree,' he said.

Ossian and Oscar followed him, skirting a great mound of earth. It was the mound Diarmuid and Grainne had made over the body of the Surly One.

'Diarmuid must certainly have come here,' said Ossian, 'but it is strange to imagine him spending the night up a tree.'

'If you say he is not here, it makes me more certain that he is here, my son,' said Finn, slapping Ossian's back. 'But perhaps I am wrong. Perhaps Diarmuid has taken my wife elsewhere. Either way, he will surely return to a place such as this. Let us wait for him.'

Finn called for his men to make a camp there, and for a gaming board to be brought. When it came, he set it down beneath the tree, sat and asked Ossian to play a game with him.

Ossian agreed. They arranged the pieces and Finn made his first move.

Up above, amid the leaves, Diarmuid and Grainne looked down on them.

They had come to visit the grave of the Surly One, whose death still haunted Diarmuid. Grainne sung for him and afterwards she suggested they eat some berries. Doing so, their hearts lightened. They danced beneath the tree, twirling and laughing, and were climbing among the branches when they heard Finn's force approaching.

Diarmuid watched as the game unfolded. He had played countless times against Finn and Ossian. He knew their styles well. Finn was the better player and was proving it now, luring Ossian into a trap before moving in for a swift kill.

'Well,' said Finn as he put down his piece. 'It has come to this. There is one move you can make that will take you out of the trouble you are in. I challenge you to see it.'

Ossian sat still, and Diarmuid hissed to Grainne, 'I know what move Ossian needs to make it, and I do not think he will see it.' Before Grainne could stop him he plucked a berry, held it out and dropped it. The berry landed and burst upon the square that Ossian needed to move to. He made his move.

'Well done,' said Finn, making his next move.

The game progressed, and soon Finn had Ossian cornered again.

'Don't,' hissed Grainne.

'Ossian is in bad straits!' replied Diarmuid.

'We are in worse ones!'

Diarmuid would not be dissuaded. He plucked another berry and let it fall. Ossian made his way out of danger.

A third time, Finn pressed Ossian. A third time, a berry fell, and this third time, Ossian's move won him the game.

'Well played, son,' said Finn. 'Though it is a shame you needed the help of Diarmuid, who hides in the tree.'

'Those berries fell as berries do,' said Oscar. 'It is the jealousy clouding your mind that makes you think otherwise, Grandfather.'

'Is it?' asked Finn. 'Well, this is easily settled.' He looked up. 'Diarmuid? What do you say?'

The camp fell silent.

The leaves parted, revealing the faces of Diarmuid and Grainne.

Diarmuid and Finn regarded one another. A full year had passed since they last met. Diarmuid was shocked by the changes in his old friend; the malice in his eyes that had never been there, through all their long years of friendship.

It saddened him to see what had become of the Fianna's Captain, whom the bards could speak of all winter without telling the same tale twice. Yet it angered him further that Finn had allowed himself to sink so low. Envy and hatred lurked in the hearts of all men. It was a warrior's duty to fight them as he would any foe.

Diarmuid was tired, too, of running. He was tired of being an outcast, when once he had been adored; and he was emboldened by the berries, which opened his heart to the love he had denied for so long.

Before the eyes of Finn, and for the very first time, Diarmuid kissed Grainne.

Slow and deep and hungry was their kiss. Compared to that kiss, the taste of the berries was the taste of mud and ash. The world became a whisper as their hearts took flight like soaring eagles.

After an age of the earth had passed, Diarmuid pulled away and looked down at Finn.

'For all that hurt me,' said Finn, 'and hurt me it did; it is nothing compared to what you did, stealing my bride on the eve of my wedding, when you were charged with guarding her. All the same, Diarmuid, you will die for those kisses.'

Finn stepped back. 'Surround the tree!' he roared.

The Fianna did as commanded, standing five ranks deep around its trunk.

'This time he will not escape,' shouted Finn, prowling back and forth ahead of his warriors. 'If one man brings down Diarmuid, all shall be rewarded. If Diarmuid is lost, all shall be punished. Death to the traitor!'

'Death to the traitor!' the Fianna shouted back.

A warrior stepped forward, Garbh of Slieve Cua. 'Let me go first,' he said. 'The honour of taking the betrayer's head shall be mine.' He ran, leapt and swung himself up into the foliage.

As Garbh crawled and leapt towards Diarmuid, Grainne saw a familiar figure appear out of nowhere to stand on the branch beside her.

'Angus!' she whispered with a smile of relief.

'You both need to come with me,' said the Son of Og. 'There is no escape if you stay.'

'Take Grainne,' said Diarmuid. 'I must remain.'

'But –'

'Go!' said Diarmuid as Garbh drew closer. 'Go to Keshcorran. I will find you there.' Before she could say more, Angus wrapped his cloak around her and spirited her away.

Diarmuid stayed in the tree, fighting and climbing higher as more and more men climbed the tree. He had the height advantage, and was full of the taste of the berries and his love. None could touch him.

Down beneath the tree, as yet another body landed, Finn's temper broke.

'Everybody! Everybody get up that tree! Kill him or I will have your heads!'

That was when Oscar, Finn's grandson, took a stand among the bodies at the bottom of the tree.

'No,' he said. 'Nobody will go up this tree. There has been enough death tonight. Finn, forget Diarmuid, and forget Grainne. It is clear to see that they love one another, and after all this, Grainne can surely bear no love for you. Let them go and the Fianna will be saved. Keep at this and we will be destroyed.'

Goll MacMorna stepped forward. 'You seem to think it your job to command the Fianna. Does Oscar call himself Captain now?'

'Ha! Goll MacMorna, telling me to respect the rule of Finn,' said Oscar. 'Every man here knows the desire of your heart. This does not concern you. Go back to your lackeys.'

Black Gary, who was a brother of Goll, stepped forward. 'We're going forward, young one. Get out of the way or I'll carve you up like meat for the table.'

Ossian drew his sword and stood between Black Gary and Oscar. More hands went to sword hilts.

Diarmuid seized his chance.

He leapt from the tree, landing among the far ranks of the warriors. Finn had spread out his men in case of such a leap. The

Fianna had been focussed on Ossian and Oscar, Goll and Black Gary; but they quickly recovered themselves, and as Finn screamed at them, they surrounded Diarmuid.

Diarmuid fought as he hard rarely fought before. He was pressed in on all sides, his sword a blur as he fought the Fianna. Their most skilled swordsmen surrounded him, pressing him just as Finn had trained them. Diarmuid cried out as he was cut. The swordsmen laughed and pressed him harder.

Diarmuid would have been killed there and then. But Oscar fought his way through to him, and soon the two were back to back, moving steadily away from the tree and its light, into the safety of the shadows.

Near the tree, Black Gary made to join the melee, but Conan held him back.

'Let Finn's friends kill one another,' said Conan. So the word spread, and the Sons of Morna hung back at the rear of the battle.

At last Oscar and Diarmuid escaped. Diarmuid led Oscar through the wood he knew so well and the Fianna gave up, seeing that their prey was lost.

In the morning they retreated to the Hill of Allen, save for those left behind to bury bodies, beneath the dancing branches of the berry tree.

THE QUARREL

Diarmuid and Oscar ran half the day, stopping only to wash their wounds.

Oscar offered to stay with Diarmuid, but Diarmuid refused him. 'It is a sad fate to live like an outcast or thief, after knowing the life of the Fianna. I would not wish it upon you.' So Oscar said goodbye to Diarmuid and made his way back to Allen, to face the wrath of Finn.

Onwards went Diarmuid to Keshcorran, wary of pursuit as storm clouds gathered in the dark afternoon sky. Walking through the woods, he spied a fire where Angus and Grainne sat together. Angus embraced Diarmuid, and asked him to bring Grainne to the safety of Bru-na-Boinne.

'The only thing that could follow is war,' said Diarmuid.

'The Tuatha De Danaan do not fear the Fianna,' said Angus.

'They should. Besides, enough death has been dealt since we fled the wedding feast. I will not have more lives on my conscience, be they Fianna or sidhe.'

So Angus said goodbye to Diarmuid and Grainne once more. As the storm broke over the hills and woods, they made for the Hill of Keshcorran.

Scouting the caves that line the hill, they settled on one and made their camp. They separated to go in search of dry wood, returned and made their fire. They had no furs to lie on so made do with their cloaks, which Grainne lay down side by side.

For a long while they simply sat, letting the warmth of the fire dry their clothes and warm their bones. Their thoughts dwelt on the previous night, when their lives had again changed so suddenly.

They both missed the comfort of their cabin, where they had known happiness for a short while, and wondered what danger lay ahead of them.

Yet for all that, Grainne was bursting with happiness; for at last, Diarmuid had kissed her.

As the storm screamed outside, she went to Diarmuid and sat close to him. She took his hands in hers, and looked into his eyes.

'I am sad, too, that we lost our home,' she said. 'But I am glad that we have finally found one another.' She put her lips to his. For the briefest of moments, he accepted her kiss; then he pulled away.

'I'm sorry,' he said. 'I cannot kiss you.'

'But you already have.'

'And if I live until the last setting of the sun, I will remember it. But I cannot break faith with Finn, no matter what kind of man or monster he has become.'

'What about me? I know what you shared with Finn; don't we share something? Do you not love me?'

'Please, Grainne. No answer I give will make things better.'

Grainne drew back. 'Tell me, then,' she said, her voice cold. 'If you do not love me, and are only here because of the bonds I put on you; why did you kiss me?'

Diarmuid hung his head as he said, 'I was angry at Finn. I was drunk on the juice of the berries. I –'

But Grainne had heard enough. She turned from him, took her cloak to the far side of the fire and lay down to sleep.

No sleep came to either of them.

It was in the darkest hour of the night that a visitor came to their cave.

Diarmuid and Grainne were both lying on their cloaks, staring at the flickering shadows cast by the fire, when a deep, grating voice called out a greeting.

They leapt to their feet. Diarmuid grabbed his spear and held it ready to throw.

There was the sound of footsteps. A shape among the shadows.

Into the firelight walked a Fomorian.

This one was not a giant like the Surly One; but he was two foot taller than the tallest man, with a thickly muscled frame, sharp teeth and a high, thick brow. He wore skins that smelt of the sea and was carrying a curragh, a skin boat.

'Forgive me for the intrusion,' he said with a leering smile. His eyes rested on Grainne awhile before he looked at Diarmuid and spoke again.

'I am Ciach. I was travelling between the islands of my people and lost my way amid the storm. I come seeking shelter, until the storm abates and I can go west again. If I may share your fire, I promise to be a graceful guest.'

Diarmuid did not like the look or feel of Ciach, nor did he like the way he looked at Grainne. Yet the rules of hospitality would not be broken by him, and he welcomed the Fomorian, who sat down to warm himself.

'I do not think I can sleep, with the storm so loud,' said Ciach as the thunder shook them. 'I wonder if either of you would care to game with me?'

'I would play,' said Diarmuid, who, despite his reservations about his guest, would never pass up a seat at a gaming board. 'But I have no board.'

'I do,' said Ciach. From a pouch in his belt he took a strip of leather. He unrolled it, revealing tiny strips of skin that served as pieces. Diarmuid listened as Ciach explained the rules of the Fomorian game, and soon all else was forgotten as the two of them played and Grainne watched.

Diarmuid liked the game, and played well enough. But he was new to it, while Ciach had played since he was a boy. He lay traps and Diarmuid walked into them. Ciach laughed, taunting

Diarmuid, while looking more and more often at Grainne, who did not look away.

Ciach made his final move. The game was his.

The Fomorian threw back his head and laughed. 'Not bad for a beginner,' said Ciach. 'Not bad at all.'

'It is a fine game. I would play it again sometime,' said Diarmuid.

'I'm glad to hear it. But now,' said Ciach, 'it is time to discuss winnings.'

'I have little to give, I'm afraid,' said Diarmuid.

'Oh, I wouldn't say that. I wouldn't say that at all.' Ciach stood and walked around the fire to where Grainne sat. He sat down behind her and wrapped his arms around her, stroking her hair and her chest. 'I think I will enjoy my winnings!' laughed Ciach.

Diarmuid leapt to his feet. He was about to draw his sword when Grainne spoke.

'Don't bother, Diarmuid,' she said with a smile as Ciach's hands roved across her. 'Don't blame him for being a man, just because you are not one.'

With that a red mist descended upon Diarmuid. He unsheathed his sword and circled the fire. Ciach threw Grainne aside, his hand going to the axe at his belt, fear in his eyes; for Diarmuid would run him through before he could withdraw it.

Ciach snarled at Diarmuid as Grainne, her fury unleashed, grabbed Diarmuid's dagger, which lay by the fire. She threw herself at Diarmuid and sank the dagger into his thigh.

Diarmuid howled in pain but did not drop his sword. He ran at Ciach, swung his sword and cut Ciach's head from his body. As the body fell and the head rolled, Diarmuid stared at Grainne, blood pouring from his wound.

He ran out into the storm.

༄

Grainne ran after Diarmuid. Through wind and rain and in darkness she ran, shouting his name, stumbling and falling over and over again. She grew so cold that she forgot she was cold, so wet that she forgot she was wet; she forget everything except finding Diarmuid.

It was in the hour before dawn when the storm abated and Grainne found Diarmuid. She could no longer run now; she shambled through the grass like an undead thing. Finally she came to a river and saw Diarmuid sitting on a rock at its edge.

He didn't look at her, but at a heron fishing on the far bank that gave out a cry as she sat by Diarmuid's side.

Side by side they sat, watching the last of the storm's rain fall upon the river, and the heron that was as still as they were.

Again, it called out.

'Why does the heron cry?' asked Grainne.

'It is frozen to the rocks,' said Diarmuid.

'Why did you run from me?'

Diarmuid gave her a sad smile. 'Grainne,' he said. 'I could search a thousand worlds and not find a woman more beautiful than you. I could live a thousand lifetimes and not find a woman I loved more than I love you. But your love is a cursed thing.

'Before I met you, I was a man of the Fianna. I was foremost among them, the company I esteem above all others in the world. I defended the shores of the lands I love, and when those shores were safe, I hunted and feasted with the best men in the world.

'To have the esteem and affection of his brothers; a man needs this. To be one of the Fianna; to know that after I was gone, I would live on in the tales of the mightiest fellowship on earth; that was a hard thing to lose.

'Now my name is infamous. I will be remembered as the betrayer, the oath breaker. The once-warrior who lived like a hunted creature.

'It is because of the love you gave me that I am come to this, and have nothing to look forward to but this. It is because of your love that Finn, my friend and hero, has become a man I despise. He was the greatest of the Fianna; now I fear he will be the end of them.

He turned to face her. 'Perhaps I could have borne all that, Grainne. At times I bore it happily, because in place of what I had before, I had you. Your songs, your laughter, the silver moonlight upon your hair. Your peace at the fireside in the deep winter. Your breath, the sweetest music, when I awaken in the night.

'Yet your love is a fickle thing, Grainne. Because I try to hold onto my honour, to a shred of who I once was, you let a stranger put his hands upon you, and laugh at the tearing of my heart.' He shook his head as the heron flew away. 'It would be better if we had not met, Grainne. Better had you not given me your love.'

He turned away from her, to watch the rain fall upon the grey water.

'I'm sorry,' said Grainne. 'I'm sorry you have lost so much. I don't mention it, because I am ashamed that you have given up so much for me. But you have not lost who you are. The man I fell in love with has not changed –'

'You did not fall in love with me! It is *this* you fell in love with,' he spat, pointing at the love spot that lay under his cap. 'It is not love you feel; it is the magic of a sidhe woman.'

'What's the difference? I don't care where the love I feel comes from. I care that I feel it, and that it means more to me than anything. I have suffered too since that night, cold and hunger and fear and the pain of lying beside you, night after night, unable to touch you. Yet I have never been so happy, and I would change none of it; but for this last night.'

Diarmuid had no reply to that. They sat upon the rock until Grainne asked him if he would come back to the cave, for the rain was still falling. He agreed.

They walked back in silence, stoked the fire and warmed themselves, while outside the storm began to make its music again.

'Would you eat something?' asked Grainne. 'There is the bread and cheese that Angus gave us.'

'Yes,' said Diarmuid.

'Where is your knife, for cutting the bread?'

'It is in the sheath where you left it.'

Grainne looked among the folds of Diarmuid's cloak and saw the knife still protruding from his thigh.

It was the worst shame she ever felt, taking hold of the hilt and withdrawing the knife, watching fresh blood pour from the wound as Diarmuid gasped and grit his teeth. She helped him dress his wound, she cleaned the knife and afterwards they ate together.

After they had eaten, they lay down together, and for the second time, Diarmuid kissed Grainne. The storm sang to them all through the night, and when they left the cave, it was broken bread that they left behind them.

THE WANDERERS

Walk anywhere in Ireland today and you'll find places where Diarmuid and Grainne slept. Through deep snow and summer sun they went ever onwards across the country, as tired and desperate as wounded deer and as rich as a king and queen in their hall.

Sometimes they made crude shelters in the forest; at other times they lodged in abandoned houses. At the best of times they would find a cave to make their own. Sometimes folk recognised them, for their tale was on every tongue in Ireland by now. Some would offer sympathy and secrecy, food and lodgings; others would call them traitors and shout for their capture.

Wherever they went and whomever they met, they cared for little now except one another. Their love that had been held back for so long now flowed like a river, its source a deep, undying spring. Every night, be they on a bed of leaves or in the deepest depths of a cave, Grainne would lie awake, stroking Diarmuid's black hair and singing to him as he slept.

Sleep peacefully my love,
The birds are in their nests now,
The farmer is by his fire,
The owl is on the wing

Sleep peacefully my love,
For the heron has gone home now,
No hare lopes in the meadow,
No bees fly among the flowers

Diarmuid of the dark hair,
And the cheeks like blood on snow,
Whose heart never knew any evil
I live my life for you

So sleep in peace 'til tomorrow
Dream of mead, and music, and me,
Dream that I'm yours and I love you
And wake to know that it's true

Grainne would sing until she fell asleep herself, and if she woke
before Diarmuid, she would sing a waking song for him.

Open your eyes, Diarmuid,
The stag is on the hill now,
Dew hangs from the green grass,
The cuckoo sings his song

Open your eyes, dear one,
The fox is in his den now,
The eagle calls the sun forth,
The mists of dawn have gone

Rise and kiss me, Diarmuid,
For Finn has not forgotten us,
Wary as deer we must be,
When wolves walk among the trees

So wake to me, your Grainne,
And the spell I'll never wake from,
That gave me you, my Diarmuid,
The best man there ever was

Grainne told no lie; Finn had not forgotten them.

In his half-empty hall in Allen, where few poets stopped now, Finn would clear the room and approach the fire. Kneeling before it, he would perform divination. In the flames he might see his prey on a bed of heather; he would call to his men and have them search the hills.

In time the fire began to fail him. He put his thumb to his tooth, and saw the lovers by the sea or embracing beneath an oak. His men would search the coasts, or hunt them through the forests.

The Fianna were far fewer in number now. Finn's riches dwindled, as he paid any and every man that offered to join the hunt.

Years passed this way. One winter, Diarmuid and Grainne made a home in the cave on the Hill of Howth, which overlooks the bay where Dublin now sits.

An old woman lived in a hut on the hill. She guessed who the new arrivals were and, like many across Ireland, she favoured them over Finn. So she helped them, bringing clothes that she made for them. She visited when she was lonely, and they helped her and visited her too.

One winter day upon the hill, she saw a man out walking upon the thin snow, and greeted him. He was old and his hair was silver, yet she thought him fair.

'What brings you to the Hill of Howth?' she asked him.

'I seek a woman and her love,' said Finn.

He looked at her in a way no man had looked at her for many years. He spoke honeyed words no man had ever spoken to her, and soon she cared for nothing but to please him. She told him what he wanted to know, which was where he might find Diarmuid and Grainne.

He walked her home, and stayed the night with her, and after that there was nothing she wouldn't do for him. When he told her that he was Finn, the hero of the tales, she grew faint, and told herself she had always taken his side.

Finn left her, promising to return. She dressed and made her way to the cave, to do as he had asked of her.

'Diarmuid.'

Diarmuid looked up from the gaming board he was carving to see the old woman approaching. She was soaking wet and dripping water onto the cave floor.

'Is it raining so hard? When we went outside last there was snow on the ground, but the sky was clear.'

'On my life,' said the old woman, who had a gleam in her eye and a spring in her step that had not been there before, 'I never knew a storm such as the one blowing outside.

'Every lake is frozen over. The ice is as hard as the mountains. Even the sea is grown solid, so that an army could walk upon it. Robins are falling dead from the sky; the wind could flay the flesh from a man's bones.'

'Why are you abroad?'

'To warn you, dear lovers, not to venture outside. Stay here, and I will tell you when the storm has abated.' With that she left, and because she had always been a good friend to them, Diarmuid and Grainne believed her. They stayed within their deep cave, making their food and water last, with nothing to do but carve, sing and nestle beneath the furs together.

Meanwhile, Finn was at work.

As devoted as he was to his search for Diarmuid and Grainne, Finn was not blind to what was happening about him. His hall was near-empty; men deserted him in droves. The Sons of Morna mocked him openly, while Goll courted favour among the powerful men of Ireland.

This was it. Either he made an end of Diarmuid and brought Grainne home from the cave or his rule would fail.

Finn left nothing to chance.

He returned to Allen and sent out messengers across the country, calling every fighting man that would come to gather beneath the Hill of Howth.

On the night of midwinter, he went out under the stars alone. Finn crossed the country and came to Oweynagat, the Cave of the Cats in Connacht, where creatures who serve the Morrigan dwell.

Crawling inside, he made his way down and sat in the darkness that can only be found in the belly of the earth.

Mustering all his hatred of Diarmuid, Finn put his thumb to his tooth.

He heard the clatter of bones, and felt the breath of a wind from beyond this world. A vision appeared before his eyes; a woman who was old when the world was young. A serpentine tongue licked Finn's face, his eyes, and the spirit laughed as she learnt Finn's desire.

What price Finn paid her, it is not known; but she agreed to serve him and bring Diarmuid into death.

❧

In the cave on the Hill of Howth, days and nights had passed. The old woman had come time and again, saying that the storm had only grown worse.

'I swear it, the snow now lies so deep,' she said, 'that a tall man could reach up and touch the moon.'

One day, a scrap of her cloak caught beneath her boot and was torn off. After she left, Grainne picked it up and smelt it. She smelt the salt of the sea.

'It is not rainwater that has soaked the old woman's cloak,' she said to Diarmuid, 'but seawater.'

❧

They looked at one another, thinking the same thing.

In that instant, the cave rang to the sound of Finn's horn.

Silently Diarmuid arrayed himself for battle. When he was ready, Grainne kissed him and they went out together.

On the snowy plain between the hill and the sea stood one of the greatest armies Diarmuid had ever seen. He recognised many a former friend among the men, but most he did not know. Most did not even wear the markings of the Fianna.

Stood on a rock some distance off was Finn MacCoull, his silver hair blowing in the wind.

'Look,' said Grainne.

Upon the water of the bay, a little boat rode the gently lapping waves of the sea. Angus Og sat in it.

'One way or another, our long walk will end here,' said Diarmuid.

There was a commotion in the ranks. Oscar emerged and climbed towards Diarmuid. Shouts and threats filled the air, but none dared cast a spear at Finn's grandson.

Oscar reached the cave mouth, embraced Diarmuid and turned to stand by his side.

Finn's army shook their spears. They banged their sword hilts against their shields and cried their war cries. The first crows began to circle overhead.

'Stay behind us,' said Diarmuid to Grainne. 'Wait for Angus.'

He turned from her, roared a challenge and with Oscar at his side, charged at the army baying for his blood.

Diarmuid and Oscar fought back to back. They called on all their years of training and fighting, all the tales they had heard and lived of impossible battles won.

Oscar had no thought but to keep Diarmuid alive; Diarmuid had no thought but to give Grainne safe passage.

Thankfully, Angus came the moment the fighting began, flying over the army and seizing Grainne, carrying her to the boat that waited in the bay.

Rivers of blood poured down the hill as Diarmuid and Oscar fought Finn's army. No matter how many men they felled, more came at them.

From his vantage point Finn watched the fighting, or looked across the bay to the boat in which his bride sat. He noticed that Goll and the Sons of Morna had not come. Neither had Caoilte, nor Ossian, nor many other great men of the Fianna.

Diarmuid and Oscar fought atop a mound of bodies now. The sky was darkened by a legion of crows.

Finn's army would soon be an army of corpses. Men he had paid to fight were deserting, running for the trees.

It didn't matter. The army did not know their true purpose; to tire Diarmuid.

At last Diarmuid and Oscar's battle cries rang out and were not returned. They descended the great hill of the dead, wading through the steaming river of blood that carved its way through the snow to the sea.

Finn saw Diarmuid turn and look at him. His ageing eyes could not make out Diarmuid's expression, but he imagined his old friend mocking him, the grey Captain too withered to fight, whose bride he had stolen.

'Laugh all you wish, Diarmuid,' whispered Finn. 'If you survive what is coming.'

Finn spoke the words that he had been given in the cave.

❦

Grainne heard a ripping sound, as if the air were being torn in two. She looked away from Diarmuid, who was running across the blood-soaked snow towards the boat while Oscar made for the woods. In the sky far above, the crows not already feasting parted in panic.

They came together again, forming the shape of a woman.

❦

The wraith hurtled through the air towards Diarmuid. Grainne screamed a warning; Diarmuid looked up, saw her and fell to the ground.

Finn's summoning soared into the sky and readied to strike again.

❦

Diarmuid rose, his shoulder screaming where the summoning's dart had penetrated him. He pulled the tiny bone dart out, though his hand turned black at its touch. Looking up, he saw her circling. He aimed the Red Spear and threw, and it seemed it would strike her. But the carrion birds that gave her form parted, and Diarmuid's spear fell to the ground.

Grainne and Angus were calling. He ran, then limped, towards them as the dart's poison blurred his vision. Otherworldly voices sang in his mind, singing of his death.

Down she came again. He tried to leap out the way, but he was too slow now. Her dart pierced his thigh and brought him to the ground.

Diarmuid tried to rise. He could not.

The voices were deafening now. Death was everywhere; it was the air he breathed. He rolled over, saw her diving again and threw his second spear. His aim was true, yet could not touch her. A dart pierced his belly.

Through pain and dark mists Diarmuid watched as his killer turned circles in the sky, readying herself for her final strike.

She dived. Time slowed, and Diarmuid was almost relieved that his long wandering would be at an end.

Angus' voice whispered in his ear.

'The leaf,' he said.

Diarmuid saw that his enemy held to her mouth a rolled up leaf. Through a hole in it she blew her darts.

❦

Diarmuid shook his head. He shook off death's calling. He would not leave Grainne.

The dagger that his love had once planted in his thigh, he threw now at the spirit of the cave. It spun through the air and shot through the hole in the leaf, piercing its target.

With a shriek that never left those who heard it, Finn's summoning was destroyed. The crows dispersed and flew away.

That day was the last day of Diarmuid and Grainne's wandering. Diarmuid waded to the boat and climbed aboard. Angus spoke a spell to banish the poison from his wounds, Grainne put his head in her lap and they sailed north-east towards Alba.

As Angus rowed, Grainne watched Finn. For the first time, she felt pity for the man who stood beyond the ruins of the battle, utterly alone.

THE BOAR HUNT

It was to Alba that Angus took Diarmuid and Grainne. First they stopped at some skerries north-east of Howth, where Angus stretched Diarmuid out on the sands and worked his druid arts until Diarmuid healed.

Within the space of the day he rowed them over the sea and up Alba's west coast, where fading winter sunlight lit up the pine forests and the endless snow-clad mountains. The tiny boat skimmed the waves as Grainne held Diarmuid, speaking and singing tenderly to him, filling him with love that cast out the last shadows of Finn's summoning.

'Where will we set down?' Diarmuid asked Angus.

'In Glen Shiel, east of the Misty Isle,' said Angus.

'But Glen Shiel is close to Glen Elg,' said Diarmuid, 'where the Black Boar hunts.' Though many years had passed, Diarmuid had not forgotten Enda, his childhood friend who was turned into a boar; the creature that had been prophesied to kill him. He had heard that a huge boar, bigger than a horse, prowled Glen Elg. Diarmuid knew that this must be Enda.

'It makes no sense,' said Angus. 'And that is the sense of the sidhe; for Finn would never think to look for you there. Keep out of Glen Elg and you will be well.'

The two lovers agreed to that, for they trusted Angus and were beyond tired of Finn's attention. Diarmuid lay with his head in Grainne's lap as Angus brought them within sight of the Isle of Mists, that is now called Skye.

They passed into the sound between the Isle of Mists and Alba, then turned east, entering the sea loch that wound through Glen

Shiel. Finally they landed and stepped out of the boat, onto the pebble beach of the place that they would call home.

'Here,' said Angus, 'you can begin life again.'

꧁꧂

Angus' words proved true. Deep within the woods of Glen Shiel, Diarmuid and Grainne built a simple house and lived a simple life. When they chanced to meet their neighbours, they said nothing of their history; they were but a woodsman and his wife.

A season passed, then a year. The sorrows of the long hunt grew distant. Grainne became pregnant and gave birth to a son, then another, until four boys played in the woods about the cabin and helped their parents to thatch the roof. Snow and sun and storms came and went, and as Diarmuid and Grainne sat by the fire some evenings, talking of Ireland, their old life seemed more a tale than days they had lived.

'I wonder how things are with the Fianna,' Diarmuid would often say. 'I wonder what became of Finn.'

'I don't,' Grainne would reply.

꧁꧂

When Finn watched Grainne sail away in Angus' boat, he felt peace in his heart at last. She was gone. The hunt and all the hate it had stirred in him were heavy burdens to bear. Standing there on the rocks, watching the boat get smaller and smaller, he realised he wanted them gone. He wanted it over.

Finn supervised the remnants of his army as they made a funeral pyre of the slain. He even lent a hand himself, something he had not done in a while. They watched the great pyre burn, and gave voice to the songs that are sung at those times, and returned to Allen.

꧁꧂

There, Finn set to work on reforging the Fianna. New tests were held that brought in new blood. Feasts were announced, and Finn led the hunts to provide meat for the table, inviting the best bards to sing and play. Though he no longer had the speed a swordsman needed, in the mornings he was first up and in the practice yard, ready to instruct and encourage the new Fianna and to offer shrewd advice to the older swordsmen.

Those that had spoken ill of Finn began to speak well of him again. It was the work of years, after all the damage that was done during the days of the hunt, but the feasting hall at Allen began to fill up again at night. Bran and Sceolan sat at Finn's feet and slept upon his bed. Finn slept peacefully.

Goll, Conan and the Sons of Morna blamed one another for missing their chance to strike.

Diarmuid and Grainne's sons had all but grown up when Angus came to visit. He stayed in the house in the woods of Glen Shiel and was glad to see his friends aged and content. They shared many a tale, and eventually Grainne said, 'For all we are content here, and for all Finn has harmed us, I wonder if it isn't time to make peace.'

Angus was surprised to hear this, for she had never held any affection for Finn. What he did not realise was that Grainne was tired of living so far from the bright and busy halls of kings and lords. Grainne would not be a queen, as she had grown up expecting to be. She was at peace with that, but what about her sons? They were of royal blood; would they grow up as huntsmen and woodcutters? If peace could be made with Finn, could they not perhaps foster with the Fianna?

Diarmuid agreed. If peace could be had, he would like to have it. So when Angus returned to Ireland, he went to see Finn. Angus was feted as befitted the Dagda's Son, and when he and Finn were alone, they talked of Diarmuid. Finn agreed that the time of peace-making was long overdue.

Angus returned to Alba. He told his friends what Finn had said, and Grainne suggested that they invite Finn and his best men over to Alba for a Samhain feast. Diarmuid agreed, and Angus returned to Ireland with the invitation.

All that summer the family laboured to prepare the feast. Each made for themselves new garments; Diarmuid carved new bowls and chairs. They hunted day and night, smoking and salting the meat. Grainne went out to the ceilidh houses, seeking new songs with which to entertain her guests.

The week before Samhain, Finn and his captains crossed the Irish Sea. They rowed north up Alba's west coast and east up Loch Shiel, landing on the pebble beach. They followed the directions Angus had given them, walking over carpets of golden leaves to reach the little house where the feast awaited them.

Finn called out a greeting. The door opened, and out walked Diarmuid, Grainne and their sons.

Diarmuid and Finn smiled at one another. For the first time in many, many years, the two friends embraced.

Finn smiled at Grainne, she smiled at him and for the very first time, the two embraced.

It was Ossian's turn next, then Oscar, then Caoilte. Laughter broke out, and soon all were around the fire, whisky flowing, stories and jokes streaming forth, and if you had seen them, you would have said there never was a happier company.

Days and nights came and went as the guests went back and forth between the fireside and the rooms prepared for them. Grainne remembered how she had loved to host gatherings in her father's hall, and she felt young again as she led the company in song and saw to her guests' every need. She and Finn were awkward together at first, but the mead did its work, and they found their ease with one another as Samhain night drew near.

On that night, many a candle was lit. Finn told the story of the fire-breathing fairy man who came to Tara. The mood was joyous, but not raucous; there was more relief than celebration in the air, that the long feud was ended and friendship renewed. The next day, the company would return home, bringing Diarmuid's sons with them for fostering.

The night's peak passed. The company went to bed.

All except Finn, who, when all were asleep, put on his cloak and went out into the darkness.

Ↄ৵৽

Diarmuid awoke to the blowing of Finn's horn.

'That is the Dord Fiann,' he said to Grainne, who had awoken too.

'It is night-time. Finn cannot be hunting,' said Grainne.

'If he has blown the horn, I must go to him,' said Diarmuid.

Grainne didn't want him to go. She tried to dissuade him, but Finn's horn blew again, and Diarmuid would not listen to her. 'I am no longer one of the Fianna, but Finn is my guest, and if he is in trouble, I will help him.'

Diarmuid armed himself and left the house. The horn had sounded to the west, and that way he went by the moon's light. He left the forest and took a path towards the mountain peaks as dawn crept closer. Up and up he went, until he stood atop the rocky mountain ridge east of Glen Elg.

Finn was there. His horn in his hand, his cloak flapping in the fierce wind, he surveyed the rippling mountain peaks that stretched on into the distance like the waves of the sea.

As Diarmuid drew up beside him, Finn turned west. That way lay the ocean and the Misty Isle beyond. Between their viewpoint and the ocean was the thickly wooded Glen Elg. The glen where the Black Boar dwelt.

Ↄ৵৽

The two warriors stood side by side, looking down into the dark wood.

'It is strange,' said Finn, 'that you chose to live so close to the creature that would be your death.'

'Death sits at the right hand of every warrior,' said Diarmuid.

'And if death sits close, then so does life,' said Finn.

'Why did you blow the Dord Fiann, old friend?' asked Diarmuid.

'For you, Diarmuid. For the memory of you. You have a good life now, but not one that will inspire the poets. I do not want the last tale of Diarmuid to be the one in which you ran from your Captain, his bride at your side. Better it is said that your last adventure was into the wood there, to slay the animal that many say you are too cowardly to face.'

'They do not say that,' said Diarmuid.

'I say it,' said Finn.

The wind shrieked as Diarmuid looked down on the glen.

'I wish it were not this way,' said Diarmuid. 'I wish you had not been false with me, and had truly found forgiveness in your heart. But you have not, and so here we stand.

'I do not think I can slay the Boar. But I will not have any man call me a coward; not even a man such as you. Let it be over now, one way or the other. Goodbye, old friend. May your last seasons soften your heart.'

With those words, Diarmuid left Finn. He descended the hillside and entered Glen Elg.

Diarmuid crossed the tree line. Beside a bubbling stream overhung by hazel trees, that made him think of the fair-haired boy who tasted the salmon of wisdom, he threaded his way into the wood, spear in hand.

The wood was silent. Still. Waiting. Diarmuid fancied he could hear the trees whispering among themselves, passing the message along; saying that at last, he had come.

The stream met the river. Diarmuid walked along its bank. Hazel trees gave way to oaks that were scarred as if riven by massive tusks.

On Diarmuid walked. The boar was close now. He could feel it, like the humming in the air before the breaking of a storm.

He passed between a pair of chestnut trees and saw it.

Taller than a horse. Wider than a bull. Its tusks longer than Goll's sword. The Black Boar of Glen Elg stood a hundred paces from him.

Diarmuid searched its eyes. For his old friend to remember him might be his only hope. But if the Boar knew him, its knowing inspired no love in it. It swung its tusks back and forth and stamped upon the ground.

Slowly it advanced on Diarmuid.

The Boar roared and charged. It took all his courage for Diarmuid to stand in that spot, waiting, then leap aside.

The Boar crashed into the tree. Rising, it smashed its tusks against the tree until it toppled to the ground, then turned again to face Diarmuid.

Again it charged. Again Diarmuid waited before leaping aside. This time his sword was in his hand; he brought it down on the boar's back. It was a blade he had carried since before he joined the Fianna.

The blade struck the Boar's back and broke. Only its jagged hilt was left in Diarmuid's hand.

Diarmuid sheathed his broken sword. The Boar skidded to a halt, turned and advanced again. This time it had the measure of Diarmuid. As it ran at him it dug its tusks into the ground, ploughing up the earth before it. Diarmuid jumped, lost his footing and fell beneath the boar.

Throwing himself down flat, he let the Boar charge over him and grabbed the soft fur of its belly. The Boar howled its rage as

Diarmuid wrapped his legs around it and gripped tightly. It raced on, shaking furiously, but Diarmuid would not let go.

Out of the forest the Black Boar charged, up into the hills. Diarmuid drew his broken sword again. He struck at its belly, but its hide was too thick to pierce.

Up they went, along the mountain ridges. The roaring of the Boar echoed through the glens and over the sea as the sun rose. The ground became rockier, steeper. Diarmuid turned his head and saw that they were approaching the summit of Beinn Sgritheall.

Too late, he divined his enemy's intent.

The Boar's hooves struck the jagged rocks of the mountaintop. It thrashed there, like a pig bathing in the dirt. Diarmuid's bones broke and his skin tore as he was beaten against the rocks.

He lost his grip, falling as the Boar turned and lashed at him, its right tusk breaking him open from shoulder to hip.

The Black Boar raised its head to bellow its victory.

Diarmuid drew his broken sword.

With the last of his strength, Diarmuid rolled aside as the Boar struck again. He lunged as he rolled, piercing the great beast's eye and burrowing into its brain.

Diarmuid and the Black Boar fell. They lay motionless on the mountaintop as the wind danced over them and through the glens, singing of the battle. The waves crashed like death drums upon the rocks, far beneath the blood-soaked peak.

❧

Hours later, Diarmuid awoke and was amazed to find himself alive.

He was not fool enough to think he would remain that way long. His body was broken and twisted. Everything was faint and dim and soft, but he had a wish in him that brought him, shaking, to his feet.

Grainne. He must see Grainne again.

❧

He fell and rolled as much as walked down the mountain-side. Whenever he stopped, he saw Grainne's face again, her eyes appearing amid the blue of the sky.

Few men could have made it as far as he did in the way that he was. But even Diarmuid could not make it all the way home from the mountaintop. He entered the woods that led to his home, went to drink at the river and collapsed before he could reach it.

He passed into a death-like sleep. He awoke again and saw a figure coming towards him.

'Grainne,' he said.

But it was not Grainne.

'How went the hunt, old friend?' said Finn, sitting down beside Diarmuid.

Diarmuid opened his mouth to answer. No words came.

'Handsome Diarmuid. I used to hear that women argued over which of us was fairest. I fear your looks are spoiled, now that those red cheeks that won away my wife are reddened by your own blood.'

Ossian and Oscar arrived then. They cried out when they saw the state of Diarmuid.

'Finn,' said Oscar, 'you must heal him.'

'I must do nothing,' said Finn.

'You have the power in your hands,' said Ossian. 'Bring water cupped in your hands and it will heal him. Do it now.'

'Why should I?' said Finn.

At that, Diarmuid found his voice and spoke.

'You should,' said Diarmuid, 'because I am your friend. Because I rescued you from the House of the Quicken Trees. Because it was the love spot, and nothing else, that made Grainne love me, and because I only went away with her because she put bonds on me.

'I was always at your side, Finn. I did everything I could for you, and I only ever did that one thing against you.' Diarmuid retched, blood spurting from his mouth. 'Bring me the water.'

❦

'If you do not bring him water,' said Oscar, 'he will not leave this wood alive, and nor will you.'

Finn's shoulders fell as the will to avenge himself left him. 'Very well.'

He walked away, towards the river. Reaching it, he bent down, cupped his hands and filled them with water. As he walked back, he saw in his mind the way Grainne had looked at Diarmuid by the fire. Hatred took him again. He opened his hands and let the water spill on to the carpet of golden leaves.

When Finn returned, he saw his friend covered in blood and torn open by the boar's tusk. He had been ready to argue against Oscar, but the desire left him.

He went back to the river, cupped his hands and filled them again.

On the way back, he thought of all those years in which his bed lay empty; in which he dreamed of Grainne before awakening to find himself alone. So he let the water spill again.

'Father,' said Ossian when he returned, 'Bring him the water. He is within a breath of death. I beg of you.' Seeing Diarmuid that way and seeing the pain in his son's eyes, Finn was ashamed again.

He returned to the river, filled his hands with water and returned as fast as he could without spilling it. Just as he arrived, Ossian and Oscar gave out a terrible cry.

The water spilt from Finn's hands again.

Diarmuid O'Duibhne was dead.

They fell to their knees and cried. Even their anger at Finn was forgotten in that moment. There was only room in them for grief. Finn simply stood and stared at his dead, torn open, bloodied friend, as if he did not understand what he saw.

One by one they rose and went to find moss with which to clean the body. When that was done, Ossian said, 'Angus will know what

has happened. We should not be here when he comes.' So they left, going back to their boat and beginning the journey home to Ireland.

Grainne had not slept since Diarmuid went out. She came looking for him and soon found him there among the leaves, his body broken, flies buzzing around him. The sun and moon fell out of the sky; the earth reached up and pulled her heart out of her chest. She fell down and cried, wailing like all the banshees in the world gathered together.

After a day, or two days, or it might have been a hundred, she felt a hand upon her shoulder, pulling her up, opening her mouth, giving her water.

'This was the one night,' said Angus, 'that I did not watch over him.' Angus made her eat, and they wept together; the one time the Dagda's Son ever wept.

Grainne wished herself a warrior, that she might kill Finn or die trying. But she was not, so instead she sent her sons off into the far corners of the world, to learn fighting arts to use against him.

Angus implored her to return to Bru-na-Boinne and live there with him. She refused. Grainne wanted to live in the house she had shared with Diarmuid, to linger among memories of him. So Angus gave her gold and silver and left her there.

That winter was the hardest Grainne ever passed. She had lived many a winter running from cave to shepherd's hut to forest camp, but she had done so with Diarmuid at her side. She had never been alone for more than a day or two. Now loneliness was her life, grief her husband. It was like the sea, sometimes building into a storm in which she was tossed about, beaten and near-drowned. At other times it was a quiet, unmoving presence, stretching on with no end in sight.

In time her grief grew easier to bear. One night late in winter, she heard a voice outside her door call a greeting. It was the last voice she ever expected to hear there.

Finn had come to her.

When she didn't answer, he opened the door and entered the house. Grainne could only stare at him.

'I do not seek forgiveness,' said Finn.

Grainne stared.

'Let me grieve with you,' said Finn. 'For the hatred that took me is gone, and I loved him too.'

Finn sat down by the fire.

Grainne recovered herself. She shouted and screamed at him. She hit him, even struck at him with a knife, which he took from her. No matter what she said, he would not go. So she went out, but it was cold, and she had to come back in.

Finn stayed. He gathered wood, hunted, saw to everything Grainne had not been able to do herself, though that wasn't much. She lashed at him with her tongue and fists, but he took it all until she had no more left for him. She found herself crying beside him, and he wept too.

One night, Finn spoke to her. He told a tale of Diarmuid that she had never heard. It was more to her than all the treasures of the earth. She told him a tale he did not know, and when dawn came they had not stopped. This became their routine each evening, though it was sometimes stopped when hatred rose up in Grainne, and she had to go out into the night, or slap and punch Finn, or go alone to bed and imagine Diarmuid's arms around her.

꿍

In the last days of summer they went walking one evening. They came to a river and stopped by it.

'They say you cannot look at the same river twice,' said Grainne.

'I think we are the same,' said Finn. 'I am not who I was a year ago, nor am I the man I was before we met.'

'It is strange,' said Grainne, 'that I hated you for so long, but do not hate you now. Yet looking at the river, it is not so strange.'

'It is strange,' said Finn, 'that I wanted you without knowing you for all those years, and still want you now. Before, I wanted you because you were beautiful, and then I wanted you because you had been taken from me. Now, I want you because I love you.'

A heron landed on the far bank and tucked in its wings.

'I think I love you too,' said Grainne. 'I hate myself for it, because of all you have done to me. Yet that hatred comes and flows away, like the water. My love is like the rocks beneath, unmoving.'

They turned to one another, each remembering the face of the other when they met. Grainne remembered Finn, the silver-haired warrior dressed in wolfskins, haughty and proud yet with eyes that spoke of storm beaches, forest dawns and white deer.

Finn saw the High King's Daughter, the prize of Ireland, who had looked at him with eyes that were cool and wary. There were deep lines around those eyes now. Yet still they promised him that the world held more wonders than he could ever know.

At last, Finn and Grainne kissed, on the riverbank as the heron cried.

꿍

PART IV

THE LAST DAYS
OF THE FIANNA

THE DEATH
OF GOLL

Finn's last days had come.

They were good days. He was no longer the first to rise in the morning, nor among the last to leave the feasting hall. Many mornings saw him forsake the hunt in favour of talking by the fire with old friends, or walking through the woods with Grainne, Bran and Sceolan at their sides. He was not old enough to be past hunting, or sword fighting, or spear throwing; but nowadays he took more joy in the achievements of others than his own.

There were troubles, of course. The new High King, Fergus, was more greedy of tribute than his father, and his demands were a constant headache. Among the Fianna, some dispute or other always needed resolving. But that was the life of the Captain, and it was a life Finn loved.

As the sun shone on Finn, its shadow fell on Goll. The Chief of Clan Morna still sat in Finn's hall. Goll was older than Finn; he had fought Finn's father and lost an eye doing so. He had been Captain, until Finn came along and took that from him. The High King had given him a choice; follow Finn, or go into exile. He had chosen to follow Finn, waiting until the time was right to take the Captaincy back.

Yet that time had not come. Finn was extraordinary; Goll did not deny it. His men loved him, the people loved him and he kept Ireland and Alba safe. But every man had his weakness. Finn's weakness had been exposed the night Diarmuid took Grainne and jealousy took Finn, skewering him like meat for the fire.

Goll should have acted then. He had put things in motion, courting the local lords and currying favour with the Kings of Ulster, Leinster, Munster and Connacht. Finn fell from grace in that time, swift and far; yet something always held Goll back.

Was it fear of being beaten again? Was it the joy of watching the mighty Finn fall even further? Whatever the case, when Conan, Black Gary and his allies pressed him, he had always insisted they wait another season. Eventually the season of opportunity passed.

Laughter filled the hall. Goll had missed the joke. Finn was telling some tale of his own heroics, and the hall was full of men gazing up at Finn in awe. Goll could remember when the silver-haired Captain had been a boy, roaming the woods of Slieve Bloom in the days when Goll was Captain. He had heard the stories being told about the boy, guessed him to be Coull's son and sent his brothers to slaughter him. They failed. Had they succeeded, Goll would be sitting in the Captain's chair now. The young men would be clamouring for another tale from Goll.

Goll refilled his cup.

Was it too late?

Like Finn – and more so – Goll's best days were behind him. He knew what the poets would say of him, and in truth, he doubted they would speak much of him at all. Captain for a short while, they might say. Or, Goll was also there.

Time to go to the outhouse again. He would need to go again soon after that.

Enough. His tale need not end this way – an old man who had been famous for a while, bitter and forgetful and too sore-fingered to hold a sword.

It wasn't too late. He had strength in him yet. It was time to give the poets a tale to tell.

He would make sure it was one to remember.

᷐᷐᷐

᷐᷐᷐

Finn finished his tale. His audience applauded.

'I know a tale not often told,' said Goll, his voice carrying across the hall.

'Well, then,' said Finn, 'you should tell it.'

'It is the tale of your father's death.'

The feasting hall fell silent. All eyes were on Finn.

'I suppose you would be the right man to tell that tale,' said Finn, 'seeing as you were at that battle.'

'As was I,' said Conan, who was sitting beside Goll, a cruel gleam in his eyes.

'As was I,' said their brother, Black Gary. 'But Goll is the better man to tell it.'

'Why is that?' asked Finn.

'Because I killed Coull,' said Goll.

'It was a hard fight that day,' he continued, getting to his feet, his single eye roving the hall. 'Coull's clan fought like wolves; they made raven food of scores of my brothers.

'But not Coull. He was like a woman amid warriors; a hare among hounds. His best men guarded his front, his rear and his flanks. Not just to protect him, but to stop him from running away!'

Conan and Black Gary laughed, thumping their tankards on the table.

'But I fought my way through to him, killed his protectors as if they were lambs, then faced him down,' said Goll, lowering his voice. 'And I swear to you all, when he saw me there – bloody and with eyes full of battle madness – the mighty Coull, Captain of the Fianna, fell to his knees and wept like a woman.'

Conan, Goll and a few more of the Sons of Morna laughed. When their laughter had died away, Finn spoke.

'It is good to hear the tale of the battle told. We live in its shadow, yet it is so rarely spoken of. But as well as you told it, I cannot picture it clearly.

'Perhaps telling the tale of the battle is not enough,' continued Finn, rising from his seat and signalling for Grainne to leave. 'I say we should re-enact it.

'What say you, Goll? Shall I act the part of my father? Be mindful, I wasn't there. I might forget who kills whom.'

'I say it is high time we played this game, Son of Coull,' said Goll. 'I've always wondered how that fair face of yours would look on a pike.'

'We have twenty men for every one of yours,' said Oscar, rising to stand at Finn's side.

'It was the same that day,' said Goll.

With a roar the two sides ran at one another. Tables were upended; cups and plates were sent flying.

But there was another company present; a troupe of poets and players. As the warriors drew their swords, their leader cried out the name of a song. The players took it up, and instantly the warriors fell to the ground, sinking into sleep. As they were falling asleep, the old bard put bonds on the Fianna not to fight in that hall – else life would become dangerous for poets.

Goll woke, rose to his feet and wearily roused the Sons of Morna. He led them out of the hall and away from Allen. What he had begun, he would finish.

At Daire Tardha, the Oak Wood of Bulls, another feast was at risk of turning into a fight.

A group of Fianna who were kinsmen to Finn had been out hunting and caught a giant blue pig. This could only be one of the pigs of Manannan. The Sea God's pigs are a special kind of swine; you could slaughter and eat them in the evening, and in the morning they would appear at your side, ready to be killed and eaten again.

Somehow one of Manannan's pigs had found its way into the wood and been caught by the hunters. Evening had come, the hunters gathered at the fire and an argument broke out over whose pig it was.

Goll and the Sons of Morna entered the camp.

The men fell quiet when they saw Goll and his brothers. Though Goll was no youngster, he was rightly feared.

'Brothers,' said Goll. 'I heard your wailing a league away, and it made my ears sore.' So they told him the cause of their quarrel.

'Well, it's a good thing I'm here to settle this,' said Goll. 'Clearly the pig belongs to the Sons of Morna.'

'The Sons of Morna? What claim have you on the pig?' asked one of the men.

'A good one,' said Goll. 'We're the only ones who'll be alive to taste it.'

Goll drew his sword and thrust it through the man's heart. The others stumbled back, not believing their eyes. His brothers drew their weapons and put them through their fellow Fianna. The hunters were so shocked that they barely fought back. Moments later, every one of them lay dead.

The Sons of Morna raised their weapons to the sky, blood gleaming in the firelight.

'This is where it begins,' roared Goll. 'Go now. Find every Fianna who favours Finn. Find their friends, find their women, find their hounds.

'Kill them all.'

Berach Brec strode through her hall, giving out instructions and reprimands in equal number. She would give a feast that night, and in those parts it was said that a feast held by Berach Brec was second only to a feast of the sidhe.

As on so many days before, she glanced at the seat next to her own. That was where Finn had sat, when they were married for a time. She had loved him, and she loved him still, but he had not been happy. He was happy now, or so she heard. It gladdened her, though it pained her too.

The main door opened. Her manservant.

'Guests have arrived early, my lady.'

'Too early. Who would arrive for a feast at –'

An enormous, bald-headed man appeared behind her servant. Berach screamed as the man thrust a spear through her servant's chest, lifting him up as he twisted in his death throes and blood poured from his lips.

The bald man's eyes met hers. She knew this man. Conan.

Conan looked her in the eye and laughed as he hefted his spear towards her. The servant came crashing down on the table.

'I hear you're giving supper tonight,' said Conan. Other men entered the hall, all with the same leering look. 'I know a dish you can serve.'

Berach Brec's guests arrived later that evening. There were no guards at the gate, no servants to attend to them. Where was Berach?

They found her in the hall, along with all her servants. Some were laid out on the table, skinned and burnt, with apples in their mouths. Berach was skewered on a spit over the smouldering fires, the smell of her burnt flesh filling the air.

Carved into the wall was the sigil of the Sons of Morna.

Deep within the woods of Munster, nine young men of the Fianna approached a river pool.

It was the hour before dawn. They couldn't see the pool yet through the dim light, but they could hear music. The men grinned at one another. A few adjusted their hair, checked the sheen of their sword hilts.

Reaching the pool, they saw nine women sitting on its banks. One played a harp, another sang while another softly beat a bodhran drum. They played the music of morning, looking into the eyes of their guests in a way that could not be mistaken.

These women, who were of the Tuatha De Danaan, took turns to play and sing while the others danced with the men, or spoke words of poetry to them. When that was done, all nine women and nine men disrobed and slipped into the pool. Here, their dancing grew more intimate as shafts of sunlight played upon the water.

Goll and the Sons of Morna arrived. They surrounded the pool. They notched arrows to their bows.

The trysters saw and heard nothing until Goll gave a shout. They opened their eyes; looked up; cried out.

Their shouts were cut short as arrows pierced their hearts, binding each couple together in death.

❧

The rampage continued. All across Ireland and over the sea in Alba, news spread of the Sons of Morna's atrocities.

Finn and those loyal to him were not idle. They followed up each report, sending twenty men for every Son of Morna. One by one, the bands of rebels were cornered. Every last man fought to the death. No one wanted to take a captive or be captured. After the massacre at the pool, the Tuatha De Danaan sent fighters to aid Finn. His retribution grew even swifter.

Conan was surrounded among the rocky plains of the Burren. A dozen men died bringing him down. There is a cairn of stones there, which some say is his resting place; others say he is buried to the east of the Burren.

❧

Only a few Sons of Morna remained now.

One of them was Goll.

❦

It was on a strand by the sea that the Chief of Clan Morna met his end.

Cairell, Finn's foster son, was the one who found Goll. Cairell was travelling with a band of Fianna. He was not yet a warrior, though he was due to take the tests and showed promise.

Cairell was out scouting among the dunes, for some fishermen in the nearest village claimed to have seen the light of a campfire by night. He soon found the remains of a fire. They were carefully hidden, but not well enough to escape his eye; Cairell was a good tracker and scout.

He reached for his horn, put his horn to his lips and froze as someone cleared their throat behind him.

Turning, Cairell found himself facing Goll MacMorna.

'Are you going to blow that horn, lad?' asked Goll.

It was Cairell's only chance. Blow the horn, and keep Goll at bay until help came.

All he had to do was blow the horn.

Yet his lips would not move.

Goll laughed. 'First taste of a real fight, is it? Don't worry, son. You won't have to do this twice.'

Goll threw himself at Cairell. He knocked him to the sand and punched him savagely, filling Cairell's mouth with blood and broken teeth. The blow brought Cairell to life again. He struck Goll on the jaw with his elbow, knocking Goll's head back. Cairell wriggled out from under the old warrior; but Goll grabbed him and threw him, sending him flying through the air. He crashed to the ground and the one-eyed warrior was atop him again.

'Let's try that again, shall we?' said Goll.

❦

He punched Cairell, again and again. The world spun, the roaring of the sea filled Cairell's ears and he saw spectral men and women approaching. Though he could still feel the hammer blows of Goll's punches and the splintering of his skull, he smiled. Cairell knew that these people had come to take him over the sea, to the Land of Promise.

Hours later, one of Cairell's companions found his body.

He blew his horn, over and over. Weeping, he promised his friend that he would be back soon to burn him. Then he began the chase.

⚶

Goll heard the ringing of the horn. They were after him.

He ran up the nearest dune, scanned the horizon and cursed as another horn sounded to the north. To the east, over the plain, he could see warriors running his way.

To the west lay the sea; but there was a strand a little way to the north, a finger of rock pointing west. He would have to hide there and hope to slip past them.

Goll ran. He reached the strand and laughed, not believing his luck; for among the rocks was a cave mouth.

He entered. It was a tunnel cave, the ceiling high enough for him to walk all the way to the rear. It wasn't deep, but it would be easy to defend. Only one man at a time could attack him here.

The horns blew closer.

'Check the cave.'

As quietly as he could, Goll readied his spear.

Footsteps. Goll tensed.

'He's –' Goll cut the man short by putting a spear through his throat.

Shouts came from outside. They had him.

Goll retrieved his spear and lay the corpse across the cave to trip up

⚶

his next attacker. The man came, and Goll missed him with his spear throw. They fought with swords, and Goll made another corpse.

He made another after that, and another, until no one dared enter the tunnel. But there were men outside still, and he heard instructions being given, to summon all the Fianna that would come.

Goll sat down amid the newly dead, leaning his aching back against the cave wall.

Night came. Goll could hear the crackle of a fire outside.

Who would come? Who would dare enter? Perhaps an old hand who knew his fighting tricks; Caoilte or even Finn himself. It might be some lad fresh from the trials, relishing the chance to make his name.

Goll didn't much care. He wouldn't win fame because he fell to this man or that one. It was his own deeds that would earn him his name.

It was easy to imagine himself dead, sat there in the dark with corpses for company. Only one question could occupy a man's mind at such a time. Had he lived well? Would his name be remembered?

It was a relief to find no doubt in his mind. He had lived well. He had fought in more battles than other men had heard of. He had bedded more women than there were birds in the forest; he had emptied his cup at a thousand feasts. Though he had not led the Fianna at the end, he had been Captain for a time. No man won everything he desired. When his tale was told, it would be the tale of a villain; but better that, than to be in no tale at all.

Finally the reinforcements arrived.

Goll fought them all.

He killed them all.

More arrived. This time, Goll called out to them.

'Enter and fight if you will, but toss me a waterskin first. There is no honour in slaying a man dying of thirst.'

He heard them speaking for a while. A waterskin was tossed into the cave. Goll drank from it, thanked them and bid them enter.

It went the same as with the other men. Those remaining outside called to Goll, asking for a truce so they could retrieve their dead. He allowed it.

Goll killed all those men, and the next group to arrive. So it went, until at the end of twelve days, Goll lay down to sleep and did not awaken. He died in the cave, having eaten no food and asked for none. Though he had an appetite for bread, he had no more appetite for life.

Goll MacMorna entered the next world with a smile upon his lips. He took many there with him.

THE LAST BATTLE OF THE FIANNA

In a high, windswept place, the last of the Sons of Morna gathered.

Great was their grief over Goll. When they were done with lamenting him, they discussed their next move.

Black Gary spoke. He told his brothers that to fight Finn meant death, and so did running from Finn; for sooner or later the Fianna would find them. There was, he said, another way.

He would go to see Fergus, the new High King. He would make Fergus an offer; to aid him in destroying the Fianna. Fergus would no longer have to pay tribute and provide hospitality for the Fianna during winter; the Sons of Morna would be free of their enemies. Of course, there would be no Fianna after that; they would have to seek out their fates elsewhere.

The Sons of Morna argued through the night. In the end, they agreed to Gary's plan.

Black Gary went to see the High King at Tara.

'With the aid of the Sons of Morna,' said Black Gary, 'and all the armies of Ireland, you can defeat the Fianna. We know their tactics; we know their strengths and weaknesses. The fighting will be fierce; an ocean of blood shall be spilt. But when it is done, Ireland shall be free of the yoke of the Fianna.'

Fergus was a proud and greedy man. He resented having to fawn over the Fianna, listening to tales of their greatness in his hall where his own ancestors should surely be celebrated. Always he had an eye on his gold, and he well knew how much more he would have, were it not for the Fianna. Yet he was no fool, and knew a battle against them, even with the help being offered, was not to be entered into lightly.

'Perhaps I could summon Finn here,' mused Fergus, 'and cut off the head of the Fianna, so that the body crumbles.'

'You could,' said Gary. 'But better to summon Oscar. He is the young hope of the Fianna. Every man among them loves him, and he is better with a spear than even Diarmuid was. In time he will be a great commander, perhaps greater than Finn. If there is a head that needs cutting off, it is Oscar's.'

So Black Gary and Fergus made their plan. Gary went back to hiding in the wilds, while the High King sent out a messenger, inviting Oscar to a feast.

ॐ

Fergus was not popular at Allen, but none there suspected the depths of his treachery. Oscar accepted the invitation and set out with a party of his best men.

On the way to Tara, they stopped to rest. Oscar walked alone to the nearest river to wash the dust from his face.

Reaching the riverbank, Oscar saw there an old woman. She knelt on the far bank, washing clothes in the river. The clothes were covered in blood.

Like everyone else, Oscar knew what such a thing meant. Death was coming. But whose?

'Old woman,' he said. 'Whose clothes are these?'

The old woman looked up at him, smiled and went back to washing her clothes.

Oscar and his men arrived at Tara. They were feted with due honours, and the feast laid on for them was sumptuous. Oscar sat with his men, his spear in its holder upon his back; for he never went anywhere without it.

ॐ

The night passed in feasting and tale-telling and music, until the company fell silent as Fergus stood.

'Oscar,' he said. 'We are honoured to have the young hope of the Fianna here at Tara.'

'It is an honour to be invited,' said Oscar.

'We have much in common,' said Fergus. 'We both follow in the footsteps of great men. We must surely wonder if our achievements will equal theirs. And, we are both spear fighters.' The High King motioned to a serving man, who handed Fergus his spear. 'I must admit, I have long admired your spear. Would you allow me to hold it, to feel its heft and study its shape, if I allow you to do the same with mine?'

This was a strange thing to ask. No warrior wished to be parted from his weapon. But neither did a man wish to refuse a request of his host, let alone the High King. Oscar's mind raced.

'I would agree to that,' said Oscar. 'But since I never before did such a thing, I would only ask that you hand me your spear, before I hand you mine.'

Fergus' face darkened. 'You distrust your King?'

'I place the trust in you that you place in me,' said Oscar.

An uneasy murmuring rippled through the hall.

'You seem to think yourself my equal,' said Fergus.

'I think myself a warrior asked to give up his spear.'

'I am no longer asking,' said Fergus. 'You have insulted me with your distrust, and your claim to be my equal. Hand over your spear.'

Oscar could see his men tensing. They were ready to fight, calculating the odds. They would win a fight here; but he would not let such a thing happen, any more than he would hand over his weapon.

'I will not insult my host,' said Oscar. 'Nor will I hand over my weapon. I will go instead, and take my men with me.'

'Ha! There it is. The arrogance of the Fianna,' said Fergus. 'I am always your host, Oscar. You and all your men. You demand tribute of me. You force us to put you up in winter. The Fianna are a burden on me and on Ireland. I put up with it for the sake of my father, who like so many others, was in thrall to the Fianna.

'You are my servant, Oscar. My weapon with which to defend Ireland against invaders. Show me where your loyalties lie. I demand one last time, hand over your spear, and show that the future Captain of the Fianna is loyal to his King.'

Oscar looked around. His next words, he knew, would decide the fate of the Fianna.

'I will not.'

'Then go home,' said Fergus, 'and prepare for battle.'

❦

❦

In the darkness they travelled home. At dawn, Oscar called a halt in the same place where they had stopped on the way to Tara.

Oscar emerged from the trees on to the riverbank.

Knelt there, washing blood from clothes, was a whole host of washerwomen. The river itself ran red. Among the women sat a sidhe harper, playing the most mournful tune he had ever heard. The washerwomen sang along to it, and Oscar was afraid.

They reached the Hill of Allen. Oscar reported to Finn, who sent out a summoning to all the chief men of the Fianna. Days passed, and once they all were gathered, a counsel was held.

'It is clear to me,' said Finn, after Oscar had told his tale, 'that Fergus wants war with us.'

'Why now?' asked one of the chiefs.

'It is the Sons of Morna,' said another. 'They want control of the Fianna.'

'The Sons of Morna are at work here,' said Caoilte. 'But that is not their aim. Fergus has long hated providing tribute and hospitality to us; we would still require that, even under the Sons of Morna. I think that they seek to destroy the Fianna forever.'

'I wish I did not agree,' said Finn, 'but I do. The High King will raise an army against us, and if we do not defeat them, the Fianna will be no more.'

'And what if we do defeat them?' asked Ossian. 'How can we survive then?'

'We will speak of that after we defeat them,' said Finn.

It was agreed that they had no option but to fight. So they chose a place for the battle, on the Plain of Gabhra near Tara, and sent a messenger to Fergus. He agreed to the place, and named a day, and the Fianna set to work on their battle plans.

∞

∞

The sun would stay behind the clouds that day.

Drizzling rain fell on the fields where the two armies were encamped. Finn and Grainne stood among the trees on the hill above their camp.

Wisps of fog drifted across the plain. Among the camps, men walked here and there; warriors on guard duty and those who could not sleep. Very soon the horns would blow and call every man to arms.

Across the plain, he saw sigils from all over Ireland scattered across Fergus' camp. How many in that army truly hated the Fianna, truly wished to fight them? It did not matter. They were here, and fight they would.

Finn voiced the thought that had kept him awake through the night. 'Is all this my fault?'

Grainne had been waiting for him to ask.

'No,' she said. 'Though of course you will think it. This is the way of nature. All things are born; they have their hour in the sun; they come to an end. The Fianna are no different.'

'But Ireland needs the Fianna.'

'New protectors shall arise.'

'And if they don't?'

'Then a new people will take Ireland, just as our people took her from the Children of Danu, and they took it from the Firbolgs before them.'

Finn was about to reply when a horn blasted, answered by a hundred more.

'It is time,' said Finn.

The two forces faced one another.

At the front of the royal army, Black Gary stood with Fergus. He had already spoken with the Kings of Ulster, Leinster, Connacht and Munster, as well as their chief men. The battle plan was clear.

'Men of Ireland!' cried Black Gary. 'You know what is at stake here. So do the Fianna.

'For an age of the earth they have held Ireland in their thrall. They have taken your sons for spear fodder; they have claimed your gold and your silver; they have stolen the hearts of your wives. The Fianna say they fight for Ireland, but in truth they are too busy fighting each other. Finn is called generous, brave, the best man that ever lived; yet he murdered Diarmuid, his closest friend, and took Diarmuid's wife to his bed.

'They know what is at stake here; their own tyranny. They will fight for that tyranny; and whatever else may be said of them, the Fianna know how to fight.' Black Gary paused. 'Yes. The Fianna know how to fight. My question is: do you?'

The royal army roared back at Black Gary. They beat their swords on their shields as Fergus grinned.

Oscar addressed his men.

'I know you see the same thing I see. Fergus has five times as many men as us. Maybe ten times.

'We all know that a man of the Fianna is worth ten other men. But Fergus has a weapon we have not seen before.

'He has our own men across there with him. The Sons of Morna, our brothers who betrayed us. The High King is glad of that. He knows it will dampen our hearts, weaken our sword arms. When we see the Sons of Morna run towards us on the battlefield, we may find ourselves thinking, why fight for the Fianna? The Fianna are broken.

'To that I say, do not fight for the Fianna. Fight for Ireland. We protect her – and without us, I see a sorry fate for her.

'I see that those who come after us will not love her as we do. They will not hunt in the glen, nor listen to the song of the cuckoo. They will not visit with the sidhe, but will mock them or forget them. The halls of these men shall become their worlds; the wild places, their enemy. The Fomorians shall overrun them, and if they do not, it will be because such men are not worth fighting.'

Oscar raised his spear.

'Will you fight for Ireland?'

Stood among the Chiefs, Finn looked around as his army answered Oscar. He smiled. Finn did not see a future for the Fianna, but Oscar did, and that gave him hope.

༼ꙮ༽

The call to battle rang in the air.

Oscar's force roared as they ran at the royal army, which charged to meet them. Among the royal army, men that had been raised on tales of the Fianna saw their childhood heroes charging at them, spears aloft.

They clashed together. There was no fighting in formation in those days; it was warrior against warrior, single combat. The great men of the Fianna and the youngest recruits crossed swords with lords, farmers and fishermen.

The Fianna fought more skilfully. If there was a better fighting force in the world, no one there had heard of it. But Fergus and Black Gary knew this, and planned to bring down the Fianna by weight of numbers. They had brought to the battle every man they could find. Fighting was tiring, even for the Fianna; and there were always fresh adversaries for them to face.

The morning wore on. Countless men died; countless men took their place. The Fianna fought for survival, for Ireland, for all they held dear. Yet their hearts were troubled, for they did not believe they should be fighting at all. Fergus' men fought because they had been forced to, or because jealousy and hatred had been

༼ꙮ༽

stirred in them. Their hatred turned to naked fear before the death dance of a Fianna swordsman.

It was a sorrowful battle, but there was no turning away from it. Both sides fought on and on, the royal army always bringing in fresh men, the Fianna finding new reserves of strength.

Their strength came to them best when they looked to Oscar. He was always in the thick of the fighting, wearing armour of burnished gold that shone even on that dim day. His spear cut though his enemies like a scythe through grass; he spun like a druid dancer in devotion to death. Always he called encouragement to his men; his voice and the sight of him gave them hope.

Black Gary had a plan for Oscar.

He knew how the Fianna loved Oscar. He knew that Oscar was not only the Fianna's head; he was the Fianna's heart.

Black Gary had a plan to cut out the Fianna's heart.

Oscar cut down every man he faced. But the problem was not with the men he faced.

The problem was the men behind him.

Every man in the royal army had been given an instruction: to wound Oscar from any side, in any way they could. As Oscar swung his sword at an enemy, a spear struck him in the back. When he spun around, a sword was thrust at his side.

At first he was taken off guard. He took many blows in this way, and soon bled from many wounds. Yet he adapted so that he always kept moving, never showing his back to anyone for long. But no man can defend on all sides indefinitely; not even the young hope of the Fianna.

Oscar bled. The more he bled, the more he slowed. He stopped thinking about killing his enemies; he thought only of survival.

Those facing him sensed it. They taunted him as his golden armour ran red, a dozen spears pushing him back and forth.

It was then that Fergus found him.

Fergus's men stood back. The High King had kept to the rear of his army with an honour guard about him. He was untouched.

'Oscar,' he said. 'I believe I asked to see your spear.'

Oscar snarled as he aimed his spear at the High King.

'Come now,' said Fergus, 'it's clear you won't have any use for it soon.'

'Take it,' said Oscar.

Faster than the eye could follow, Oscar threw his spear. It was the last time he would ever throw it.

It sailed through the air as Fergus threw his own spear.

Oscar's spear struck Fergus in his face.

Fergus' spear struck Oscar in his stomach.

A roar went up as they fell to the ground. It rippled across the field, and was taken up by all.

Oscar is dead. The High King is dead.

Every man on the field fought twice as fiercely after that; the Fianna for love of Oscar, Fergus' men for fear of them. The Fianna could not be stopped. Soon their enemies were dead or running from them.

⚜

The birds of battle descended as the Fianna gathered around Oscar.

Though the ground was strewn with their fallen comrades, all gathered to mourn Oscar. In him had rested their future. They had won the battle, but their future was lost.

Finn and Ossian knelt at his side, stroking his bloodied face, tears pouring from them. It was as if the sky had been cut open, the rocks and the hills. All the world bled and as Oscar died, the Fianna died and their world with them.

'Farewell to fighting,' said Finn. 'Farewell to feasting, and poetry, and every good thing I ever knew.'

⚜

As for Ossian, Oscar's father, the best poet in the world; he had no words.

What became of the Fianna after that day?

There is no one answer to that question. There are a few more stories, which we shall hear next. But they only speak of a few of the Fianna.

They do not tell us what became of Finn.

Some say he died in in Alba, near a place called Killin. Others say he did not stand over the body of Oscar, but fell too on the battlefield that day.

One tale has it that many years later, after the War of the Brown Bull and the coming of Vikings and Christians, a smith was out walking when he found a door in a hillside, with a lock but no key. He went home and made a key, brought it back and opened the door.

Down a passageway the smith walked. At the foot of the passage, deep within the earth, he came to a vast chamber.

The chamber was full of sleeping warriors. Scores of huge men in finely wrought armour lay with sword and shields and spears beside them.

In the centre of the chamber lay one man fairer of face than all the others. The smith hardly dared wonder. Could this be ...?

At the side of that man lay a horn.

The smith picked it up. Stroked it.

What would such a horn sound like?

He blew it. It was a better sound than he had ever heard, and it made his head swim with images of battles, feasts and people more beautiful than any he had seen.

It made the men around him stir.

The smith leapt with fright, the horn falling from his lips as the sleeping warriors shifted and grumbled.

He waited. They were still again.

One more time wouldn't hurt. More softly this time.

He put the horn to his lips and blew again.

The warriors stirred. This time some stretched, while others rubbed their eyes. A few even opened their eyes and looked at him.

The smith was terrified. He dropped the horn with a clatter, ran back up the passage and out the door. As he slammed the door shut behind him and locked it, he heard a cry from the chamber.

'You have left us worse than you found us,' the warriors cried.

The smith never returned. The Fianna went back to sleep. Some say that when Ireland or Alba are in their greatest need, the door shall open, the horn shall be blown and Finn and the Fianna shall arise to fight again.

The thought makes for a fine ending. But there is still the story of Ossian.

OSSIAN & NIAMH

In a green glen on the island of Rathlin, the last of the Fianna had gathered.

There were only a few dozen of them. While most forsook arms for the plough or sought their fortunes in foreign lands, a few went back to the old way of the Fianna. They kept away from kings and great halls; they took shelter in caves and on lonely shores.

Among them was Finn's son, Ossian. As the cold evening came, Ossian sat alone by his fire, fletching an arrow. So intent was he on his task that he did not notice when everyone in the camp fell silent.

Finally, Ossian looked up.

A woman on a white horse had ridden into their camp. She wore a circlet of gold and a gown of silver and starlight. She was looking at Ossian.

'I am Niamh,' she said. 'I have ridden here over the ocean, Ossian, and I have come for you.

'My home is Tir Nan Nog, the Land of the Ever-Young. There, people dwell in peace and plenty. We hunt white deer through evergreen forests while in the air, bright-winged birds sing. Every home is a palace and every evening we feast, dance and sing, deep into the star-bright night. No one grows old or speaks ill words; none say this is mine, that is yours.

'I have crossed the waves for, Ossian. Your words are of such beauty that they are spoken even in our halls, and through them I have come to love you. So return with me, Ossian. Be my husband and live forever in the land all hearts yearn for.'

It was a tempting offer; but Ossian was unsure. He had fallen in love with Niamh the moment he laid eyes on her, but he was a man of the Fianna. He was one of the last of the Fianna, and no men ever had such strong bonds as the ones gathered in that glen. He looked around the camp. Could he forsake them?

Looking into Niamh's eyes again, he knew that he could, and he would. He was a poet. Where his heart went, he would follow.

Ossian said goodbye to his brothers and climbed onto the back of Niamh's horse.

They rode away, out of the glen and across the island. When they reached the sea they rode over it, their steed gaining speed as it galloped over white waves. Ossian held on to Niamh and laughed as he had not laughed in a long time, while Ireland disappeared behind them.

Through the night they rode, and through the next day; for three days and nights they rode. At dawn on the fourth day, the sea surged and a storm blew up around them. Ossian looked left and right, and out of the crashing waves and swirling mists came ghostly shapes and apparitions. Glittering cities in worlds never heard of; nightmare creatures in lands that knew only darkness. Beautiful beings called to him; shadowy wraiths screamed and –

'Eyes forward,' said Niamh.

Ossian pulled himself back, focussed his gaze forwards and in that moment, the storm abated.

The mists parted. The sea became as still as glass, and Ossian looked upon the white shores of Tir Nan Nog, Land of the Ever-Young.

Up the shore they rode and through green forests until they reached the palace that would be their home. They dismounted, passed through the gates and began their life together.

Everything was just as Niamh had promised. The people of Tir Nan Nog were beautiful and peace-loving. They sang songs to praise the sea and stars, the forests and shores and one another. They drank only wine and crystalline water; every night's feasting was better than the last. Ossian was made welcome, and loved for his heart and words. He loved Niamh ever more deeply, and wrote never-ending verses in the rapture of her beauty and grace. They danced, laughed and lived without cares; they rode through the high glens, faster than the wind.

Ossian lived in peace, perfection and plenty until, after a time beyond time, he began to feel rather bored.

Nothing ever changed in Tir Nan Nog. Nothing ever went wrong; no hunt ever failed. No one ever made a crude jest; the feasting never ended in a good fight. Ossian found himself yearning for bad weather, grumpy men and surly women. He wanted to hear filthy jokes. He wanted to stumble out of the feasting hall and vomit down his fine clothes. Such things didn't happen in the Land of the Ever-Young.

Ossian wanted to see Ireland and Alba again. More than anything, he wanted to see the Fianna.

Once these feelings awoke, they would not rest. Ossian went to Niamh and told her that he wished to go back, just for a short while, to see his friends and brothers and homeland. But to his surprise, Niamh would not have it.

'Do not go back,' she said.

'Why not? I will return,' said Ossian.

'You will not,' said Niamh.

'Of course I shall,' said Ossian. 'I will only be gone a short while. I am a man of the Fianna, and it is no small thing for us to be parted from one another; especially after all that has befallen us. Let me go.'

'Don't go,' said Niamh, and though he pressed her for a reason, she would not give one.

Ossian gave up and went on with his life, but everything had changed. What had been wondrous now was dreary; when he looked at his wife, no verses sprang from his lips. She was no longer the one who had brought him there; she was the one who kept him there.

In time, moved by the depths of his despondence, Niamh said to Ossian, 'Very well. Take my horse. Go back to Ireland and see your brothers. But come back to me, and beware. You may not like the world as it is now.'

Ossian was overjoyed and barely heard her warning. 'Yes, yes,' he said. 'Of course I'll come back.'

Very soon he was sitting atop Niamh's horse, ready to depart.

Niamh said to him, 'Listen to me carefully. If you remember one thing, remember this. You must not get down from the horse. If you do, if your foot so much as touches the tips of the grass, you will not return here, and I shall not know happiness again.'

'There's nothing to worry about,' said Ossian. 'Goodbye, my love. I'll return soon.'

Ossian rode away, leaving Niamh weeping behind him.

༺ঞ༻

East across the sea he rode. Storms rose up and fell away; Ossian never glanced left or right. He never ceased smiling nor singing as he raced home, towards Ireland, Alba and the Fianna.

Three nights and days passed. On the fourth morning he saw the sun rising ahead of him and beneath it, the shores of Ireland.

On to the shore and over the sands of Kerry he rode. Ossian whooped and cheered as his horse trotted through the dunes and up into the hills. Atop the hills, he surveyed the land and felt all the joy of homecoming. The hills and woods were singing a welcome

༺ঞ༻

to him and he could not sit still, knowing his brothers were somewhere out there.

Down from the hills and into a village he rode.

Something was wrong.

The people were small, thin-limbed, drab and mirthless. In the muddy village square they gathered around and stared up at him, the gold-clad warrior on his white horse. Most of them drew a curious sign in the air, crossing their hands over their bodies.

'My friends,' said Ossian, 'where can I find the Fianna?'

They laughed at him, shook their heads and scurried away into their little houses.

Ossian travelled on to another village as clouds rolled in from the west and a steady rain began to fall. It never rained in Tir Nan Nog.

It was the same there, and in the next village.

'You're Ossian? From the stories? Ha! Wait until I tell –'

Enough. Something was very wrong and Ossian was frightened. He needed answers, and there was one place he would be sure to get them.

Ossian rode east, all the way across Ireland. Night had fallen when he emerged from the woods and rode up the Hill of Allen. Here, surely, he would learn the truth.

He reached the top of the hill.

Finn's shining white fort was no more. All that was left were heaps of broken stone amid the long grass.

Ossian's heart broke. He climbed down from his horse to walk amid the ruins of his home, his world …

Too late, he remembered.

Ossian, Little Deer, the last of the Fianna, gasped and fell to the ground as his legs gave way beneath him, the life poured out of his bones and his flesh greyed and sagged.

A man out hunting rabbits for his pot found him there the next morning. He saw an old man, white-haired and twisted, drooling and raving about Finn, Oscar and other men from the old stories.

The old man was so small and frail that the huntsman could pick him up. He carried him home, warmed him by his fire and brought different people to speak to him and try to get sense from him.

'A madman,' they said. 'Thinks he's Ossian, from those pagan stories.' But where did he come from? Of the horse, they said nothing; for it had turned and galloped away the moment Ossian's foot touched the ground.

Yet he spoke with such conviction of the Fianna and their battles. He knew nothing of the world; he claimed to have never heard of the gospel.

Eventually, it was decided. A few days later, Finn's son opened his eyes to find a stranger studying him from across the fire.

The man introduced himself as Patrick.

He held a wooden cross in his hands.

OSSIAN & PATRICK

In the house of Patrick, Ossian learnt how the world had changed.

The Fianna and the sidhe were long, long gone. A whole age of the world had passed. The strange, small, sad people whom Ossian had encountered on his return from Tir Nan Nog ruled Ireland now.

His coming was not celebrated. The people did not run from house to house, exclaiming that the Son of Finn MacCoull was among them. Finn, Angus Og, Manannan; those names were forgotten now. Anyone who knew them spoke of them with sneering laughter. Tales of the old world were superstitious nonsense at best; the dark work of the Devil at worst.

Yet there he was.

Many in that house called him a madman. Others thought him some ghoul sent by their Devil, to toy with their minds and interfere with their good work.

As for Patrick? Whatever nonsense he believed, he was made of stouter stuff than the rest of them. He did not fear Ossian, and seemed to enjoy talking and arguing with him.

'Well,' said Patrick to Ossian one day, 'what clouds are passing through your mind today, keeping from you the sight of God?'

'Enough of gods and clouds,' said Ossian. 'I have earthly things on my mind today. I need more to eat. Is it any wonder my sight is failing when I am given such wretched rations?'

'You are given a quart of beef, a churn of butter and a loaf of bread each day,' said Patrick. 'That is more than some here get by on.'

'Of course it is! Your people are like mice next to the men who walked the earth in my day. I am surprised you need more than crumbs to keep you alive. I swear I have seen a quart of a blackbird, a rowan berry and an ivy leaf bigger than your quart of beef, your churn of butter and your loaf of bread.'

'Ha! No matter what my people say of you, I will always enjoy having you around, Ossian,' said Patrick, rising to leave. 'Your nonsense makes me laugh like a child, and I am reminded that we are all children in the eyes of God.'

Patrick left the room.

A short while later, Ossian rose from his chair and reached for his cane.

Slowly he made his way through Patrick's house until he met a serving boy.

'You,' he said. 'Take me to the kennels.'

༺༻

Arriving at the kennels, they saw a bitch with a litter of pups.

'Go to the kitchens,' said Ossian to the boy. 'Get a leg of meat, bring it here and nail it to the wall.'

The boy did as he was told, and when that was done, Ossian said, 'Bring the pups. Throw them against the leg, one by one.'

Ossian squinted to see as the boy brought the pups, leaving the mother howling in her kennel. He threw them one by one at the meat. Each of them fell, until the last pup was thrown. It held on with its teeth and claws.

'Keep that pup,' said Ossian. 'Put it in a dark place, and never let it taste blood or see sunlight.'

'What about the others?' asked the boy.

'Drown them,' said Ossian.

༺༻

ぐ§ఏ

The boy did as Ossian asked. After a year, Ossian came to see the pup. He was well pleased with it, and called it Bran Og; Young Bran.

'Come, boy,' said Ossian. 'We are going to take Bran Og out hunting.'

They donned their cloaks and set off into the forest. Bran Og tore back and forth ahead of them. Ossian leaned heavily on the boy.

At the forest's edge, Ossian stopped as he spied a rock covered in ancient markings. He told the boy to look under it. The boy did as commanded and found hidden there a horn, an iron ball and a dagger.

'Blow the horn, boy,' said Ossian.

The boy put the horn to his lips and blew. He had never heard a sound like it.

'What do you see?' asked Ossian, gripping the boy's shoulder. 'What do you see?'

'I don't see anything.'

'Nothing?'

'No. Except a dark cloud …'

'They are coming!' said Ossian. 'Watch this, boy!'

The cloud on the horizon began to draw near. The boy saw that it was not a cloud but a flock of birds, black and bone-beaked and screeching. The birds were as big as the biggest hounds in the kennels.

The birds landed in a nearby field. Bran Og howled and raced towards them and soon had one of the birds between his jaws. The rest took to the sky and flew away screeching.

'He caught one!' said the boy, proud of the pup he had raised, but his joy was short-lived.

'Be ready with that ball,' said Ossian.

Moments later, a change came over Bran Og. He turned towards them, dropped the bird and ran at them, dark foam pouring from his mouth.

ぐ§ఏ

'Kill him!' cried Ossian.

'But he's my pup!' said the boy. He was terrified of Ossian but he loved the pup dearly.

'He'll kill us!'

The pup was almost upon them. The boy could see from the look in its eyes that it meant to tear out their throats.

He hurled the ball at Bran Og. It flew into the pup's open mouth. The pup that had been reared in darkness fell down dead.

'Take the sword now,' said Ossian.

The boy held back his tears as he obeyed Ossian's instructions. He cut open the bird and withdrew from its stomach an enormous berry and an enormous leaf.

That evening, Ossian presented to Patrick a quarter of a black bird bigger than his quarter of beef; a rowan berry bigger than his churn of butter; and an ivy leaf bigger than his loaf of bread.

Patrick shook his head and made the sign of the cross. He still would not increase Ossian's rations.

✼

Ossian lived out his days in Patrick' house. They were friends, though for every hour they spent in companionable silence, they spent a dozen hours arguing.

'Tell me, friend,' said Patrick, settling into his chair at the fireside one evening, 'was today the day you chose to repent?'

'Repent for what?'

'For sinning, old man! For a lifetime enslaved to the pleasures of the flesh, in thrall to women and feasts and bloody battles, without a thought of Christ and Heaven!'

'Do not start on your Christ again, I beg you. Let us speak of someone less dull.'

'There is nothing dull about the Son of God, who was sent to deliver us from evil.'

✼

'Well, your God never sent him to Ireland, did he? And just as well! Angus would have had his head. Or, if he really was all you say, he would have joined the Fianna!'

'The Fianna, the Fianna,' said Patrick. 'Will you ever tire of talking of them?'

'Before I met you, I never met a man or woman who did not wish to speak of the Fianna. If you had seen us on the field of battle, shaking our spears at the frosty dawn, you would have begged to join us.'

'But I did not see them, did I? Nor will I ever see them, if God has mercy on my soul; for the Fianna – every one of them – are in Hell.'

'If they are in Hell then they must like it there,' answered Ossian. 'Else they would have killed your Devil and torn Hell down. He could never have bested Caoilte, or Oscar, or Diarmuid.'

'You do not understand how foolish you sound. You are blind in your eyes and blind to God too.'

'Good! I do not want to look upon such a joyless character! I have my memories of Alba, her high mountains, the wolves howling in the forests as the silver moon rises.'

'A fine picture. But if you had just a glimpse, the tiniest taste of Heaven –'

'Have you been there?'

'Of course not!'

'Then what do you know of it? For the last time, I want nothing of Heaven, and I want to hear nothing of Heaven. Is Bran in Heaven? Or Sceolan? Or are they sinners to?'

'After all I have tried to teach you, you are asking me if there are dogs in heaven? No, my friend. There are no dogs in Heaven.'

'No hounds! Then what kind of man would go there? Please, spare me more of this talk. I have had enough of your dreary God and his mirthless Heaven, where men do not fight and hounds do not beg for scraps beneath the table.

'Yet you think of nothing else,' continued Ossian. 'And why? I think I know why; you are afraid. You and all your miserable flock. You are afraid of life, afraid to truly live, so you sit indoors and dream of a world where there is neither fire nor ice, loving nor fighting, hounds nor battle. You love death; the Fianna loved life.'

'They did,' said Patrick. 'And how did that work out for them?'

And so it went.

Eventually Ossian lost his sight entirely. His good humours came less frequently after that, and Patrick's followers and servants feared to enter the room where he sat muttering.

Behind unseeing eyes, Ossian lived among memories. He would take hold of a memory of Finn, Niamh or Oscar, and live it over and over. It became his way of life to dive ever deeper into his memories, trying to taste the mead of his father's hall, the sweetness of Niamh's kisses, the summer rain on a Connacht shore.

He would waken from sleep, or fall into sleep, and reach further back. In rare moments he found himself in the glen where his mother had raised him. He would nestle into her soft fur, knowing nothing of good or evil, Heaven or Hell.

It became hard to tell which memories were true and which were imaginings. No face came clearly to his mind; his father's name eluded him. Was that Patrick across the fire from him, or was it Caoilte? That barking; was it Bran, back from the hunt? He would have to tell Oscar about Patrick and his God.

No. Bran was dead, Oscar was in Hell. Nonsense, he would be out of there by now. Oscar would be coming soon to take him from this wretched place. Oh, how he longed to see Niamh again.

So ends Ossian's tale, and the tales of Finn and the Fianna.

It is not a glorious end, but maybe it is not the end. The Fianna may be asleep under a hill somewhere, ready to rise again. Or perhaps they sleep not under a hill but in our hearts, urging us to drink ever more deeply of the cup of life.

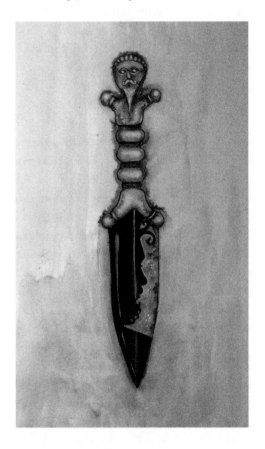

AUTHOR'S NOTE

I hope you enjoyed getting to know Finn and his men. It was a wonderful experience for me to write this book, as I got to know the Fianna far better than I had previously. I'm very excited by the prospect of introducing the Fianna to new readers. What's even more exciting is the idea that after reading this, you might go out and tell these stories. Please, please do so. That's what keeps them alive.

If you enjoyed the book, I have good news for you; I have others available that I think you'll enjoy too. My debut novel is called The Shattering Sea. It's the first book in The Orkney Cycle, an epic fantasy set across Prehistoric Scotland and Scandinavia. You can download it as a Kindle or Kobo ebook for free.

I have a fortnightly podcast, House of Legends, on which myself and some of the world's best storytellers tell our favourite myths, legends and folktales. I'd love it if you subscribed, which you can do here: www.houseoflegends.me/podcast

If you'd like to tell stories yourself, I have a membership site for storytellers called The Roundhouse, where you can develop your skills within an active and supportive community. You can learn more at www.roundhouseschool.com. I also offer coaching for storytellers, which you can learn about at www.houseoflegends.me/story-coaching.

If you want to write your first novel – and are absolutely, totally committed to doing so – you can get in touch with me about book coaching here: www.houseoflegends.me/contact

I have a readers club, called the House of Legends Clan. By joining you'll be the first to get news on the podcast, books, retreats and live events. As soon as you join, you'll get my free ebook,

Silverborn & Other Tales. Find out more here: www.houseoflegends. me/landing-page

If you feel like emailing me to say hello and discuss magical spears, please do so; I love hearing from readers. And please do review the book on Amazon. Reviews help me and they help other readers.

Daniel Allison

SOURCES

The following texts were consulted in the writing of the book:

Campbell, David, *Out of the Mouth of the Morning* (Luath, 2009)

Campbell, John Francis, *Popular Tales of the West Highlands Volumes I–IV* (Amazon Media)

Campbell, John Gregorson, *Waifs and Strays of Celtic Tradition Vol. IV* (Leopold, 2016)

Gregory, Lady Augusta, *Lady Gregory's Complete Irish Mythology* (Pyramid, 2014)

Heaney, Marie, *Over Nine Waves* (Faber & Faber, 1994)

Macpherson, George, *The Old Grey Magician; A Scottish Fionn Cycle* (Luath, 2016)

Montgomery, Norah, *The Fantastical Feats of Finn MacCoul* (Birlinn, 2009)

Nagy, Joseph, *The Wisdom of the Outlaw: The Boyhood Deeds of Finn in Gaelic Narrative Tradition* (University of California Press, 1985)

ACKNOWLEDGEMENTS

First and foremost, a huge thank you to Lally for running your eagle-like eye over my earliest draft and providing so much useful insight.

Thank you to Donald for your foreword and for encouraging me to turn this idea into a reality.

Craig, Aimee, Liz, Mira, Chris, Grainne, thanks for putting me up while I travelled and researched the stories.

Sean, thank you for the coaching that helped transform my life while I wrote this. To Jesse, Liz, Mon, Cassie, Pok, Steve, Nop, Julia, Aimee, Simon, Baow, Craig, Alex, Christina, Mamma and everyone else at Diamond Muay Thai, thank you for the blood, sweat, tears and hilarity.

Nicola, thank you for taking a chance on me and for your warmth and kindness.

Katherine, thank you for the beautiful illustrations; the best I could have hoped for and so much more.

Mum, Peter, Rachel, Paul, Maia, Florence, The Other One, thank you for your support in everything.

Daniel Allison

House of Legends Podcast

If you loved *Finn & the Fianna*, you'll love *House of Legends*. It's a podcast on which I tell my favourite myths and legends; the kind of dark, beautiful, weird and brilliant stories that fill this book. I also use the podcast to keep readers up to date with my new work and upcoming live events.

You can subscribe at Apple Podcasts here: https://podcasts.apple.com/gb/podcast/house-of-legends/id1463264216

On Spotify here: https://open.spotify.com/show/59C6P4JKydqe UoWYhILZBU

On Stitcher here: https://www.stitcher.com/podcast/daniel-allison/house-of-legends

You can also listen on my website at www.houseoflegends.me/podcast

ABOUT THE AUTHOR

Daniel Allison is an author, oral storyteller, podcaster and book coach from Scotland. He writes fantasy as well as retellings of myths and legends. Daniel has lived in India, Nepal, Uganda and Thailand and now divides his time between Scotland and Thailand. He loves cats and hates celery.

You can keep up to date with Daniel by subscribing to his podcast, writing to him via his website or by joining the House of Legends Club at www.houseoflegends.me/landing-page

ALSO AVAILABLE FROM DANIEL ALLISON

The Shattering Sea

In Iron Age Orkney, two races stand on the brink of war.

The finfolk have summoned an Azawan, a creature of nightmare, and the Orkadi are powerless to stop it. Talorc, whose family were slain by the demon, and Runa, Princess of the Orkadi, set out to destroy the Azawan. The secrets they uncover will change their world forever – if they live long enough to share them.

The Shattering Sea is the first volume in 'The Orkney Cycle', Daniel Allison's fantasy series set across Prehistoric Scotland and Scandinavia. Fast-paced and rooted in Celtic myths, it is perfect for legend-lovers of all ages. It is available in paperback and as a free Kindle and Kobo ebook.

'A tremendous read … no end of dramas, surprises & reversals of fortune … a rattling good plot … wonderful stuff'
Fay Sampson,
Guardian Children's Book Award-nominated Author

Stay up to date – join the House of Legends Club at www.houseoflegends. me/landing-page